STARTING, GROWING, AND
MULTIPLYING YOUR MISSIONAL GROUPS

MISSIONAL COMMUNITIES LEADER GUIDE

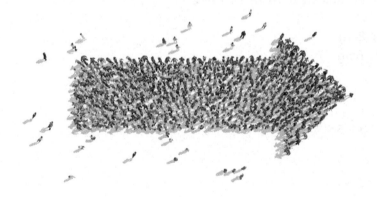

ERIC PFEIFFER

MISSIONAL COMMUNITIES LEADER GUIDE
© Copyright 2016 by Eric Pfeiffer

First printing 2016
Printed in the United States of America
1 2 3 4 5 6 7 8 9 10 Printing/Year 16 15 14 13 12 11

Cover Design: Blake Berg
Interior Design: Pete Berg

ISBN: 978-0-9965300-9-5

Table of Contents

Preface..i

A Note from Experienced Practitioners v

PART 1: BEFORE YOU BEGIN 1

Purpose of this Leader Guide.....................................3

How to use this Leader Guide....................................5

What is a Missional Community (MC)? 7

UP, IN, OUT — A Way of Life 11

    MC Rhythms Unpacked 12

    Up & In Rhythms 12

        Eating...13

        Thanksgiving 15

        Singing 16

        Family Devotion or Small Groups 17

        Prayer/Debrief...20

        Closing the MC (On Time!) 21

    In & Out Rhythms..22

        Discovering Your Mission Purpose 23

        Everyone Likes a Party 25

        Helpful Tips for the IN-OUT Rhythm 27

Leading a MC..31

    Up — Spiritual Parenting....................................31

In — Predictable Patterns...33

Out — Missional Purpose 34

More Helpful Tips for Leading a MC.....................................35

    Invitation & Challenge 35

    Building a Family Takes Time 37

    Support & Accountability 38

    Leaders Create Culture..38

    From Mechanical to Lifestyle 39

    Practice Makes Better...40

Practicalities of MC life 43

    Home Size...43

    Geography 44

    Meeting Times 44

    How often should we meet?...45

    Communicating with our MC...45

    Numbers & Attendance: Who vs. How Many 46

    MCs are seasonal...48

    Finances: Should we be tithing to our MC? 49

    Kids: What do we do with out kids? 50

    Who should we be inviting to our MC?...............................52

How to Start a MC — Laying a Firm Foundation 55

    Select Your Team...55

    Disciple your Team..55

    Train your Team 56

    Can we start a MC without a Core Group?...........................57

    Transitioning preexisting groups into MCs 57

    Starting MCs in a Church Setting 59

Assessing, Growing and Reproducing your MC........................61

Knowing if you're Winning — MC Assessment.....................61

Expanding your Circles 64

Reproducing your MC — Building the Future! 65

PART 2: 1 YEAR MC FRAMEWORK............................... 69

How to Use this Framework.. 73

MC Framework At-A-Glance 75

A Balanced Life (Intervals 1—3) 83

MC Assessment Exercise 151

Finding Fruitfulness (Intervals 4—6) 153

MC Assessment Exercise 217

The Empowered Life (Intervals 7—9)............................ 219

MC Assessment Exercise 279

Engaging God (Intervals 10—12) 281

MC Assessment Exercise 347

APPENDIX 349

Small Group Activities for UP/IN Gatherings 351

Template MC Outlines 352

Growing your UP.. 369

Growing your IN.. 370

Growing your OUT.. 371

Missional Purpose Activity Sheets 374

MC Assessment Exercise 387

Preface

A few years ago, while tending the 3DM table at an Exponential Conference, a pastor approached me with a serious situation. He explained that he had heard about Missional Communities and then researched and secured all the best resources available at the time on MCs. His church launched eight MCs on the back end of a fantastic eight week series on the missional life. Sadly, nine months later these MCs had denigrated back into glorified small groups.

"I know we need more than small groups," he said. "I know we need to develop our missional capacity to reach the world around us. I know this all happens best from the context of community and we believe MCs are the best way forward. But we just don't know how to do it."

I could see both frustration and desperation in his eyes. I encouraged him, "Rich, it sounds to me like you folks have done the best you know, but I think there's still something missing that is critical for your team to learn this new lifestyle." I went on to explain, "MCs are great in theory just like marriage and children. We've heard from others about how amazing they are and deep down inside we hope it's true. We've heard how they'll change the world and how we can participate in that blessing, but it only takes a bit of experience to discover they're also really, really hard."

MCs are not another church program, but instead a lifestyle, and lifestyle changes take a lot of hard work. It's difficult to expect an MC leader to know how to do what they've never done before. We often say that if the lifestyle of Jesus was easy everyone would be doing it!

"Then what's our hope?" Rich shot back. We've been to every conference, read every book and have spent hours praying and strategizing with little success. We don't know why it's not working."

I knew what I would say next might frustrate Rich even further, but dared to share with him one of the most precious pearls of wisdom I've received in my own journey of learning how to walk with God. "Rich, you have accumulated lots of great information and my guess is it's all good. Sure, there are a variety of nuances to how different organizations tackle MCs and they all have their own strategies about starting, growing and multiplying MCs, and here's the kicker — they all work! I know that because they're all speaking and writing out of their own stories of struggle and success."

"Rich, you need more than good information; you need an opportunity for imitation. You need regular access to leaders who have a track record of leading MCs with stories of success and failure, battles and breakthroughs; leaders who have journeyed down this road and can turn and share what they have learned. This kind of reference point will provide you with the encouragement, perspective and training so you can at least make new mistakes. You need a MC Coach!"

The guide you hold in your hand is not the only way to explore MCs, but it is a way and it's basically our way. This guide offers information on the basic tools, principles and practices for engaging in MC life in any context. But we know you need more. To ask you to figure it out just by reading this book is like asking the disciples to know how to follow Jesus just by reading a book. This journey requires an imitative opportunity. You deserve more than just good ideas and some printed resources. You need MC Coaching.

I am so thankful for the many people who have served as coaches for various areas of my life, whether it be in sports, marriage, bible study, raising kids, budgeting finances, etc. We don't expect you'll be able to successfully lead a MC without some helpful coaching. For this reason we are now offering MC Coaching for anyone who wants to benefit from this kind of partnership. We believe you can lead a MC and we want to help. Whether it's with 3DM or another coaching organization, don't underestimate its importance.

We strongly encourage you to explore how to receive this kind of support and accountability to give you the best fighting chance to start and lead a great MC experience!

Sincerely,
Eric

A Note from Experienced Practitioners

We can still remember the day we hit a wall. We had been hosting nearly 50 people in our home each week, sharing in meals, conversations, prayers, and thanksgiving. But how did we know if we were doing it right? Together we had transformed a trash-filled vacant lot in our neighborhood into an urban farm and made quite a splash. But now winter was coming, and we were facing a long stretch of Monday nights spent indoors. How would we do mission in the snowy winter?

This is when it hit us that we had no idea what to do next.

The book you're holding did not yet exist, and all the materials we could find at the time on how to lead a missional community were fuzzy on the details of what we were supposed to do as we gathered week in and week out. Were we just supposed to keep eating together every week and wait for some magic to happen? We didn't really know.

Our early experience with leading a missional community was a bit like coming across a bicycle for the very first time. The bike was shiny and seemed simple enough. It had an elegance to it, and something in our souls told us this was how we were meant to travel. So we picked it up and gave it a go. As it turns out, it's easy enough to start moving, but finding balance is extremely tricky! It took us years of trial and error to work out how to ride the bike of family on mission with any sort of balance between the Up, the In, and the Out. After all the effort it required, we could hardly imagine handing the bike over to someone else who had no idea how to ride it.

It has been said that missional communities are the training wheels that teach us how to live life as an extended family on mission. We're sure that everyone holding this book in their hands has a clear understanding of the purpose of training wheels. We all know why they're helpful and how they're meant to be used. We also know that over time, as we grow in our confidence and ability to lead missional communities, we'll no longer need them. Our job, then, is to pass these training wheels along to the next generation of aspiring cyclists as they step into their own adventure.

Recently we pulled up stakes and moved our family to Fort Wayne, Indiana, where we joined the staff at Grace Gathering. We oversee missional communities and spend most of our time training these leaders. It's important for us that our family is leading by example.

Long before we arrived in Fort Wayne, we began praying that the Holy Spirit would go before us and pave the way for a missional community in our neighborhood. God delivered. Within weeks of our arrival, we found four other families who were willing to embark on this journey together. We had a better idea of what we were doing, but how would we multiply our leadership in others?

It's important that everything we do provides a simple and repeatable example for others to follow in the future. We've learned in our leadership journey that others will only repeat what they can first imitate! As we began meeting together, we simply followed the tracks laid out by this leader guide and communicated clearly to our new community the simple patterns of life together that you'll find in these pages. Would it work? Would others be able to learn from us as we learn to lead a missional community?

That question would soon be put to the test. In our first attempts at leading a missional community, we worried about being gone on a missional community night. How could we ask someone else to try leading when we didn't know what we were doing ourselves? This time around we wanted it to be different. We wanted to begin giving away opportunities to grow in leadership almost immediately. We wanted to provide a simple example and then invite others to give it a try. That's how people learn to ride a bike, right?

The first opportunity came just four weeks in, when we and our girls had to miss our missional community gathering for a school concert. Our family loves MC night, so we were sorely tempted to switch meeting nights so we didn't have to miss a week. But that would work against the predictable nature of our gatherings. So we reached out to one of the other couples we believed might one day lead their own MC and invited them to lead in our stead. We reminded them of the simple pattern we were following and asked if they'd be willing to lead the family while we were gone. This was their exact response:

"Sounds like a good plan! We are up for the task!"

What?! We had known this couple for only a few months and they had no previous experience with missional community. After only a few weeks, they knew exactly what we do together and were up for leading it without us. In such a short time, they had already picked up on the predictable patterns of our gatherings and felt confident enough to give it a go. Having this tool has made our life as missional community leaders infinitely more multipliable.

After years of training, coaching and a great deal of trial and error, we are confident we can navigate the waters of leading missional community without this guide--but we use it anyway. We use it and will keep using it because it makes multiplying our lives as spiritual leaders a whole lot simpler. We know exactly what to do next, and now, our next generation of leaders does too.

Andy and Gina Dragt

Part 1

BEFORE YOU BEGIN

Purpose of this Leader Guide

In this guide, we aim to provide simple, repeatable, concrete steps for groups of people who are embarking on the journey of learning to live as Missional Communities (MCs), which can also be called Families on Mission. These are people committed to being the incarnational presence of God in every area of their lives, but understand the important reality that **we're better together**.

There are many definitions, philosophies, and approaches to the Missional Community life, and we want to acknowledge at the beginning we offer a way, not **the** way. We strongly encourage you to glean from many different sources and integrate what you learn with the basic framework offered in this MC Leader Guide.

This guide is meant to be like a set of tracks to run on, tracks that will create helpful rhythms on which you will invariably build. It also leaves lots of room for flexibility, innovation, and contextualization. Most people do not start something new for fear they will head in the wrong direction, or for a lack of knowing where to begin. That's exactly what this guide provides: a start in the right direction. We will provide simple, predictable patterns that are imitable and reproducible.

Leading a MC requires lots of on-the-ground training, much like raising children. No one is a great parent from the beginning. Parenting, like MC leading, is a process of leaning on your past experiences, learning from many resources, those who have traveled the path before you, and lots of experimentation. You'll use the same techniques here.

"Anything worth doing is worth doing poorly until you get better."[1] Building and leading a family of people who will learn to live the missional life together takes time and lots of patient perseverance, but it's worth it!

Notes

_____
_____
_____
_____
_____
_____
_____
_____
_____
_____
_____
_____
_____
_____
_____
_____
_____
_____
_____
_____
_____
_____
_____

---

[1] G.K. Chesterton

How to use this Leader Guide

This guide is comprised of 3 different sections:

   Part 1 introduces you to many of the things you need to know before launching into this adventure.

   Part 2 is the practical week-by-week framework for your MC gatherings that will take you through a year or longer depending on how often you meet.

   Part 3 includes resources we believe will be helpful to you through your journey.

Take time to read through the entire guide, which will give you helpful perspective as you walk the week-by-week journey. We highly recommend gathering a core group who will form the nucleus of your emerging MC and going through this guide together. It will give you an opportunity to process through many of the important questions you will need to sort out as you begin to invite others into the mix.

This is the kind of guide you highlight, underline, write in, and turn into your personal reference for your journey of learning to lead a Missional Community.

We highly recommend reading **Leading Missional Communities** by Mike Breen and **Family on Mission** by Mike & Sally Breen[2] as accompaniments to this guide. There are many theological, biblical, sociological, and ideological issues

---

[2] We'll refer to these as LMC & FOM going forward

---

explored in those books that we cannot discuss in detail in this guide. This book is meant to be a practical guide to living out the principles explored in those books.

Remember this is a framework to help you chart a course in the right direction. But just as there are various parenting styles and approaches to building and leading a family, there is freedom within this framework to explore your own preferences, passions, and practices.

This is not a prescriptive set of rules and laws to follow. There are many factors that go into leading a successful MC, but we are confident this framework provides a generous expression of many of the best practices we've accumulated over many decades of launching, leading, and multiplying MCs in various contexts.

Notes

_____

_____

_____

_____

_____

_____

_____

_____

_____

_____

_____

What is a Missional Community?

What they are NOT...

A MC is not just another program

Programs can be a wonderful delivery system for information, training, and care, but MCs ARE NOT PROGRAMS. MCs are meant to be the incubator, cocoon, greenhouse, and training wheels for the lifestyle that God created every human being to enjoy—operating as God's divine family on the earth representing his kingdom mission.

Programs generally run for a specific time and also focus on a group of particular aims, where a MC is meant to be the context in which we can grow and mature as members of God's family and learn to take on greater and greater responsibility. An MC, though structured, requires more organic flexibility and interaction than programs generally provide.

A MC is not a smaller church service, Bible study or small group

Most people will default to what they know when they find themselves in unknown territory. Many have been so conditioned by what they have experienced through the many typical church activities (e.g. Weekend services, Bible Studies, Sunday School, Small Groups, etc.) and will naturally seek for MCs to fit what they have known before. Resist this temptation. All of these other offerings are great for the purposes they serve, but they do not generally deliver on the purposes of MC.

It is possible to transition an existing group (i.e. small group, life group, etc.) into a healthy functioning MC, but it will require lots of patience and perseverance on account of what may amount to significant culture shifts. It's not required, but we recommend seeking the help of a certified 3DM Coach or other leader with experience in this area. A little bit of good outside counsel may save you lots of time and frustration.[3]

What MCs ARE...
Being the Church vs. Doing Church

Human creation began with a God who made Adam and Eve and blessed them to be fruitful and multiply, to reproduce the image of God's family everywhere they spread (Genesis 1:26-28). This is God's design. Before we were called to be Christians, we were created to be human beings. Before we were called to be the Church, God gave us the key vehicle that would help us function and flourish as humans—family. That's why, no matter how dysfunctional families become, we keep trying to figure it out.

The family of God will gather in different sizes with different purposes. Missional Communities are designed to help us to rediscover the midsize gathering, ranging from 15-50 people, both blood and non-blood related, learning to live the life of Jesus together. These families may encompass singles, families, old, young, diverse ethnicities, races... you get the picture. Anyone who has been alive more than a few hours knows it's hard. For this reason God gave us extended family because **together we are better**.

> **God gave us extended family because together we are better.**

---

[3] 3DM Coaching contact info

These midsize communities are essential because they are small enough to care (benefits of a small group) and large enough to dare (benefits of a large congregation). There's a reason many college students join fraternities, sororities, intramural sports teams, clubs, etc. They are looking for extended family even while they may be distant from their blood-related extended family. They are looking for an environment that will provide support for their needs and encouragement to succeed.

MCs are meant to help us learn how to BE the Church rather than GO TO or DO Church. They help us to stop doing mission FOR God and to start doing mission WITH God! Jesus came in part to show us the WAY of BEING the church in everyday life!

Missional Communities begin with spiritual leaders who decide to invite others into the way they are learning to be God's family on mission in their context.

Extended families have always been the cornerstone of virtually every society since the beginning of creation. It's hard-wired into human DNA, and we have a unique opportunity to help people rediscover what they are hardwired for.

Notes

You can't bring a family into something you aren't doing.
Will you come to learn how to follow Jesus with us?
We are trying to learn how to integrate our life into
living on mission w/ Jesus-
Vision-casting in laymen terms.

Notes

what are our predictable patterns of
UP, IN, OUT?

Meeting people where they are + taking them to where
Jesus wants them to go.
Invite no more than 8 people into core. 3-8 people

UP, IN, OUT — A Way of Life

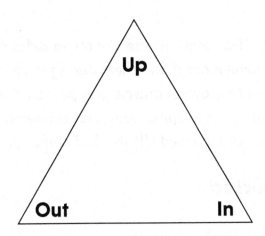

In **Building a Discipling Culture**[4], we look at how Jesus lived an integrated life, attending to the three key relationships humans are created for:

    UP: our relationship with God

    IN: our relationship within God's family

    OUT: our relationship with God's world

Better Together: Notice the emphasis on OUR relationship upward, inward and outward. God created us to live life in community therefore these dimensions of life are best pursued within the larger context of extended family life, not on an individual basis.

As Jesus led his own family on mission into this integrated life, so every MC should reflect a pursuit of the UP, IN, OUT dimensions of life together.

Life is about seasons, so remember that in any given season your emphasis

---

[4] BDC — Triangle

may lean into one of the dimensions more than the others. At the same time we should remember that it's important to grow in all three dimensions at all times.

Balance: The UP, IN, OUT dimensions are like the muscles of the human body. You may work some more than others during a trip to the gym, but it's important to make sure to grow all muscle groups intentionally. We've all seen the guy at the gym with a huge upper body and chicken legs. Avoid that look! Our MCs need to be a well balanced UP, IN, OUT community.

MC Rhythms Unpacked

Rhythms: We are recommending a healthy rhythm of UP & IN as well as IN & OUT gatherings to help your MC grow well in all muscle groups. Below we unpack simple, repeatable patterns for both rhythms. When in doubt, imitate what we offer until you feel comfortable to innovate. These rhythms are meant to help you lay tracks to move you in the right direction, but we fully expect you to recalibrate along the way based on the particular needs of your MC.

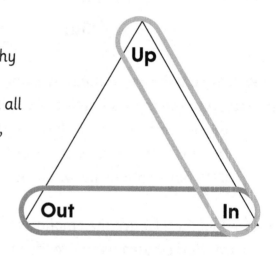

UP & IN Rhythms

UP & IN RHYTHMS — These rhythms are drawn from what we see from the snapshot Luke offers us about how the early church functioned within

Special Note:
When we don't know an answer to something about functioning in MCs, it's best to ask what a family or household would do, not what we do during a weekend service.

their families on mission (Acts 2:42-47). They were committed to the simple disciplines of the apostle's teaching, fellowship, breaking bread and prayer. The byproduct of this Spirit-filled community was powerful—they began to live selflessly, saw the presence and power of God in many ways and many came into the family! As we engage these same kinds of disciplines together in a Spirit-filled community, we will also experience the power of God in us and through us.

We recommend 1.5 hours for the official gathering of your UP & IN gatherings, using the following rhythm:

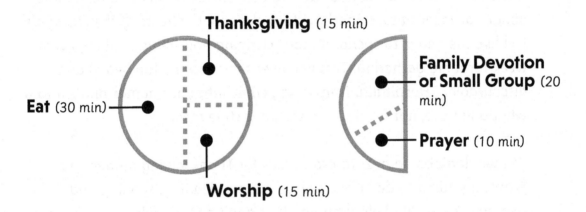

Thanksgiving (15 min)

Family Devotion or Small Group (20 min)

Eat (30 min)

Prayer (10 min)

Worship (15 min)

Eat (30 minutes)

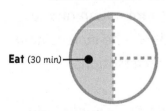

Eat (30 min)

Meals matter: It has been said if you take the stories of meals and mountains out of the Bible, there would be little remaining. Meals are an essential activity for families in every context in every generation. Meals are the place where everyone has to put their weapons down and share in a common experience that encourages conversation and vulnerability.

Lightweight & low maintenance: Whether you host a potluck, grill hot dogs and burgers, or enjoy leftovers, the most important things are that you eat together and keep the mealtime lightweight and low maintenance. In the same way that you don't have amazing meals every night at your own dinner table, don't expect that every MC meal will be amazing. We have often created a Facebook page for our MCs so we can communicate the dinner plans each week.

Hospitality redefined: People don't feel like they're family with you until they have to eat from paper plates, find their own cups, help take out the trash, and sit on the floor during their meal. We need to be honest about our meal culture and how to make sure the hosts of the MC don't feel like they have to spend an hour cleaning house and cooking every week for a MC gathering. This will over time become too heavy and discouraging. Hospitality is inviting people into your homes and sharing what you have, not hosting a restaurant style meal.

You wouldn't all go over to grandma's for Thanksgiving dinner and expect grandma to do all the prep, cooking, cleaning, serving, and cleanup. You would help grandma by bringing food, helping cook the food, coming early to set up chairs, serving the food once it's ready, clearing the table, etc. MC works the same way.

Highs and lows: Encourage folks to share how their weeks have been with each other. We often encourage everyone to share a high and low from the past week. Over time, as comfort grows, it will be increasingly difficult to pull people away from their mealtime conversations.

Kids: Let the kids eat in the same way as they would at a Thanksgiving or holiday gathering. They may need some child-friendly food, but often they can eat what the adults have. After many stained carpets, we generally have required the kids to eat over hard surfaces if they can't be at a table, and outside is the best option! Sometimes we have an adult stand by the desserts to offer the kids ONE dessert. Otherwise, they would load up on sugar, and MCs would get VERY interesting. Again, as with many questions about the logistics of MC, use your common sense.

Thanksgiving (15 minutes)

Thanksgiving (15 min) Transition to a time of thanksgiving. This should happen even while people are finishing their meal. Some may have come late and just fixed their plate, and that's OK. Gather people as best you can given the space you meet in, even if people are only in earshot.

Invite people to share quickly one thing they are thankful for since the last time you met together. These should be short, quick and concise thanksgivings, whether it's finding a lost sock or healing from cancer. They all count. The more you encourage these, the more your people will develop a culture of thanksgiving.

Don't underestimate the power of thanksgiving. Jesus says in Revelation 12:11 that we overcome the enemy by the blood of the lamb and the word of our testimony. These testimonies are our way of celebrating who God is in our lives. This also causes others to hope that, if God did something for you, then maybe he can do the same thing for them. For you salespersons, this is word-of-mouth marketing. Jesus invented it!

Kids should be highly encouraged to participate. It will be tempting to dismiss their sharing as less important or futile, but over time you will find they often lead the way in openness, vulnerability, and honesty. It is very important to demonstrate value for what the younger folks bring to the table; otherwise, they will slowly slip into complacency and begin to believe they have nothing to offer the family. In other words, take your kids seriously.

Keep the thanksgivings moving. The leaders will need to provoke the more quiet and limit the more talkative. Sometimes you will have to leave the awkward silences to give the introverts or shy types an opportunity to think and/or muster the confidence to share. I often find myself saying, "Alright everyone, let's share what we're thankful for. Big or small, everything counts. Let's make them simple and quick. Go!"

Something we have found helpful is to leverage a thanksgiving for a future blessing. If someone shares how they have been blessed in some way, we'll often ask if anyone else would like God to do that for them. Then we ask the person who shared the testimony to pray a short blessing over those who desire the same.

We have discovered that in early gatherings, most folks are a bit more timid and reluctant, but after some months of meeting, people begin to feel safe and familiar, and it can be difficult to stay on track with everyone sharing. That's a good thing!

Singing/Worship (15 minutes)

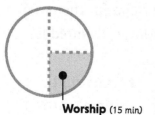

Worship (15 min)

Singing together is a very important tradition passed down through generations of God's family on earth. Humans love singing! At ballparks we sing "Take me out to the ballgame." At concerts we scream at the top of our lungs the lyrics of our favorite music group. At the beginning of our favorite sitcom we sing along to the theme song. In the car we find ourselves singing even if we don't know the lyrics to what's playing on the radio. Music has a powerful effect on us, and so do the lyrics we sing. Singing together is one way we reaffirm who and whose we are.

The greatest temptation is to think we need a professional worship leader to enjoy singing together. What do we do if no one fits the bill? Remember, we're learning to be family. We're not trying to impress people, but instead to make room for the different members of the family to learn how to contribute what they have to offer and even to learn new skills to bless the family.

Style & methodology: It doesn't matter if someone leads a few songs on the guitar, piano, or a capella, or whether you play songs on a CD player or even via YouTube. (My friends at Victory Point Ministries in Holland, Michigan, showed me how powerful this can be.) Whether you sing hymns or contemporary songs, whether you sing songs or read poetry or psalms, and even whether it sounds good or awful, the most important thing is that you commit yourselves to some form of worship on a regular basis.

Family Devotion or Small Groups (20 minutes)

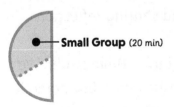

Small Group (20 min)

You will see in the MC Framework in Part 2 that we suggest a rhythm between small group time and family devotions. Both are valuable, and therefore we encourage some kind of rhythm between the two. We suggest more small group activity so that we do not put any unnecessary pressure on the MC leaders to teach. But as we have stated, it is a good idea to imitate what we have offered and then recalibrate as the Lord leads.

Family Devotions

Family devotionals are an opportunity to set the vision and values for what it means to be part of God's family on mission. This activity helps us connect the family to the UP dimension, which will shape the IN and OUT dimension.

Family devotions are an opportunity for leaders of the family to share from the family book (the Bible) what they are learning about what it means to participate in God's family on mission. We recommend these family devotions be short and simple (no longer than 15 minutes if possible).

We strongly encourage giving emerging leaders within the MC opportunities now and again to share a family devotion. The only way others will learn to do this is by watching us and having opportunity to try it themselves with helpful feedback and affirmation. As we will discuss later, one of the purposes of leading a MC is to multiply your MC, which requires you train others to do what you do. Remember, part of building a discipleship culture is providing simple, predictable, imitatable patterns others can carry on.

We recommend the devotional be about 15 minutes, followed by five minutes of open reflection from the group. We invite our community, young and old, to engage by asking questions and sharing reflections.

You may experience the temptation to turn a MC into a Bible study. We highly suggest integrating scripture into the MC experience, but doing it in a way that is simple and imitatable. In other words, the true test of whether you are utilizing scripture well in a MC is whether the people of your MC begin to integrate what you are doing into the rhythms of their own households. We often find our folks sharing how they have begun to do family devotions during breakfast or dinner in their own homes because they wanted to carry what they are learning in MC into their own home.

Kids and the Family Devotion

If you are going to keep the kids around for the Family devotions (something we recommend you do often), then it is a good idea to share the devotion in a way that is sensitive to all ages. Encourage the kids to ask their parents to explain to them things they don't understand.

There are times when we want to address the adults of the family, in which case we'll send the kids off to play at that time.

Remember, if the kids can't understand the devotion, it's likely the adults won't either.

Small Groups

Small groups are a time for the family to learn how to care for each other intentionally, attending to the IN dimension of the family.

We encourage folks to break into groups of 3-4, find a bit of space around the house, and jump into sharing and praying.

We often offer a half sheet of paper with 3-4 questions (found in the appendix) that makes engagement in the small group simple and easy. This also allows for small groups without an official leader.

We encourage new folks to jump in with the person they came with.

We encourage everyone to share and pray for each other, but also to make room for those who are uncomfortable to pass if they choose. We have often had people who are exploring Jesus or have never learned to pray aloud in our MCs. We encourage them to give it a try, but not to feel pressured beyond where they are willing to do.

Interestingly, many of the physical healings we have experienced in our MCs have been at the prayers of those whom others would have considered non-believers. As they took a step of faith and put their hope in a God who loves to heal and bless, amazing things happened!

Kids & Small Groups

Depending on the age of the kids, you can encourage them to engage in the small group activity. As our kids have grown, we have enjoyed engaging small group time together with them.

At times it will be more appropriate to send the kids off to play.

In many of our MCs, we have invited the older kids to lead the younger ones, and have generally seen this work very well. Sometimes we ask the older kids to help watch over the younger kids during this time, and other times we have found there may be an adult or two who feel called to hang with the kids during this time.

Don't be afraid to experiment in this area. The goal is to grow as a family, not have an ideal MC experience.

Debrief/Prayer (10 minutes)

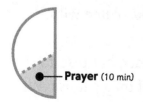

Prayer (10 min)

Leaving 10-15 minutes at the end of the formal part of the MC gathering allows for two things:
1) Time to hear from the small groups anything the larger family should know about (e.g. healing, breakthrough,

celebrations, frustrations, sickness, disease, other needs)

2) Time to pray for the sick!

We are aware that we're all on unique journeys of learning how to make room for God's supernatural healing power. Our habit (predictable pattern) is to ask who is dealing with any kind of physical (or other) malady and take a few minutes to pray for them. We ask people to surround those in need for a few minutes of prayer.

Prayer in MCs: Our simple philosophy of prayer in MCs is to encourage everyone to pray short, simple prayers simply asking God, our Father, for what we want. Jesus says, "ask, seek, knock." When we're first introducing prayer into our MC, I often say to the group, "When we pray, just ask God for what you want and leave the rest to him."

Closing the MC (On Time!)

It is very important to officially end the MC at the time you said it would end for several reasons:

This helps parents of children to predict their schedules, which is really important, especially for those with very small children.

This helps those who are new to know at what point they can escape if they feel uncomfortable.

This helps all who need to get to bed or attend to other matters leave at a predictable time without feeling bad.

I often joke about this by saying that even if The Lord is descending from on high at the close of our MC, we will officially end to allow those who need to go there way. We have discovered that people deeply appreciate the opportunity to escape when needed and to stay longer when desired. This also helps to guard the balance between the organized/structured and organic/spontaneous elements of MC life.

The host of the MC will have to decide how long past the official ending the MC to let people stay. Again, it is very important to set the boundaries that honor and serve the host household.

We have found in the initial months of gathering most folks leave soon after we end, but eventually we find ourselves kicking people out late at night or asking the last person to lock the door on their way out. Again, you have to know your limits. We're all wired different and need to know our capacity for extroversion, engagement, etc. **This is really important!**

IN & OUT RHYTHMS

Two by Two: We call these IN & OUT rhythms because too often we have thought of mission through an individual lens. But Jesus never sent his disciples in groups smaller than two (even to get a donkey!) and what we see in the life of the early church is that the most powerful evangelistic engines were these **oikos** (extended family units or families on mission) functioning in such a way that compelled those who did not know God as family to want to be part of God's family. Together is better!

Though God is the source of our IN and OUT dimensions, it's also good to understand that the two basic MC rhythms hinge practically on the IN dimension. Thank God mission is something we were created to engage together.

Additional vs. exponential power: Our evangelistic efforts are not doubled as we

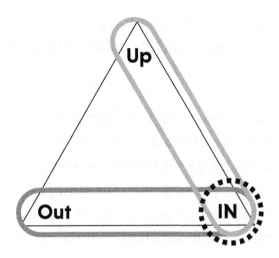

add more team, but exponentially increased. Luke is careful to make sure we know that, as the earliest MCs stumbled and fumbled their way into being the Church in their homes, neighborhoods, and workplaces, "The Lord added daily to their number those who were being saved."
(Acts 2:47)

Missional purpose and parties: We encourage MCs to develop a regular rhythm of attending to your missional purpose and throwing parties. Let's unpack each of these.

Discovering Your Missional Purpose (Once a month)

All Christians are missionaries and evangelists, but not all Christians are supposed to be like Billy Graham or move to foreign lands. Becoming like Christ means developing a missional life-style where we get to share "good news" (the literal interpretation of ***evangelize***) with others. The good news of Jesus in our lives is not only shared in word, but also in what we do. Too often we interpret the main missional power of the New Testament through the work of individuals like Jesus and Paul; however, both of these leaders were very careful to develop an extended family unit (called ***oikos***) that provided the best sustainable context from which mission can go forth. Remember, many hands makes lightens the load! If Jesus and Paul didn't engage their mission alone, neither should we.

Defining your missional purpose begins by identifying the **Passions** and **Possessions** God has already deposited in your MC to meet the particular **Problems** in the world around you. A simple exercise you can do with your MC leadership team or with the whole group is to identify the Passions, Possessions and Problems represented by your group, and then to ask the Lord where these converge. This convergence point becomes your missional purpose.

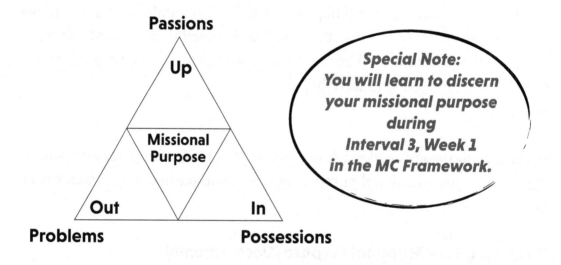

Remember, your missional purpose may shift in different seasons. We have sometimes had to experiment with a few different missional purposes before we found significant traction in one.

Once a month: We encourage MCs to be committed to attending to their Missional Purpose at least once per month. Again, we are offering simple, repeatable patterns that you can imitate, but you may recalibrate this investment based on the opportunities and needs of your missional purpose.

Everyone likes a party! (Once a month)

No one wants to be a target: It can be tempting to turn those who are not yet Christians into targets. We invite them around for Bible studies, church services and event meals where we covertly try to make them Christians. Here's the good news—you can't make anyone a Christian. It's the work of the Holy Spirit. **Our job is to evangelize people around us, which literally means to "good news" them. We good news others when we represent the heart of God by serving them as Jesus would were he in our shoes.**

Simple: Parties are as easy as inviting people to eat and play together—you don't need any major excuse. Maybe it's a birthday party, a graduation party, or a Friday party. (Yep, every Friday deserves its own party!) Just host a party, encourage your MC participants to invite their Persons of Peace[5], and have fun! We often ask a different core family or member of our MC to host one of these parties each month.

I am aware that even the phrase "let's party" has been hijacked and carries connotations of lewd conduct, unhealthy consumption, etc. We're Christians, which means we get to redeem what the world has corrupted! So, let's party in fun and healthy ways and celebrate life!

---

[5] The Person of Peace (POP) strategy is something we unpack in great depth in the chapter on the Octagon in *Building a Discipling Culture* — that reminds us that God invites us to get on board with what he's doing, not the the other way around. Jesus says over and over that he only says and does what he hears and sees the father doing (John 5:19, 12:49). Like Jesus trained his disciples, our goal in the OUT dimension is to learn to discern where God is already at work and how he has already equipped us to serve in that area. So let's focus our missional energy on people who seem to be open to us, rather than trying to beat down the doors of those who aren't. Any MC's missional efforts should be focused where God seems to be opening doors. Otherwise be open to recalibrating your missional focus as you learn where the soil is soft!

Who to invite? Here's a good rule of thumb: if I like person A, and person A likes me, and I like person B, and person B likes me, then there's a good chance that person A and person B may like each other too! We simply invite anyone who likes us (POPs) to our parties.

How to party: We often host a party around a BBQ or potluck (everyone likes food) and have games to play. Some popular games to keep people playing are Can Jam, Corn Hole (a game we learned in the midwest and have come to love), Bocce Ball, throwing frisbees, footballs, and Koob! You can host the party at the beach, a park, your backyard or at Chuck E Cheese's. Remember, the point is to make space to be with people.

How did Jesus party? It's interesting to read through the Gospel narratives and see how often Jesus was just hanging, eating, drinking, chatting, and partying with people. He shared the heart of God with a smile, a word of hope, a touch of healing, a friendly conversation, and even telling funny stories. So much of Jesus' ministry was being with those who would be with him, simply loving them as human beings, and taking opportunity to share what he had to offer. Sometimes people just needed a friend, and other times they needed to be healed from a disease. Both are equally powerful expressions of God's love. In this way the Kingdom of God constantly broke into their midst. God wants to do the same through us as we learn how to be with people and serve them, not target them. If you have the love of God overflowing from your MC, then as people bump into you, they can't help but get splashed. The question is whether what spills out of us is the love of Jesus or something else.

Interestingly, in Luke 19, Jesus was just hanging at Zaccheus' house, enjoying a good meal and conversation with those called "sinners," when seemingly out of nowhere Zacchaeus stands up, his heart overwhelmed, and begins to repent and change his life! It's helpful to remember that where we go God goes because he lives in us.

Whatever you do, **do not bait and switch**. In other words, don't invite people into what they believe will be a safe environment and then try to slip God in through lengthy prayers or with Christian paraphernalia like napkins and plates with Bible verses on them. (Yes, I've seen this before.) Leave the Testamints at home.

Helpful Tips for the IN-OUT Rhythm

Neighborhood vs. network: Your missional focus may be defined by the people who are in proximity to you (in your literal neighborhood, apartment/condo complexes, dorm or fraternity/sorority house), or in the neighborhood you spend most days in called your workplace. In our ever-changing world, we think it's important to pay attention to both the neighborhoods that are made up by geographic proximity and by relational proximity (networks). Networks may include those you work with, blood relatives, the families represented by your child's soccer team, or those involved in a particular social club or exercise group.

Start with the world around you.

As you engage your neighborhood and/or network of relationships, be on the lookout for where you can make the world a better place. Does someone need help painting their fence, moving house, caring for kids, affording car repairs, food for their bellies, mowing the lawn, prayer for sickness, etc.?

Jesus tells us to pray that God's "kingdom come on earth as it is in heaven." That's amazing! God wants the world today to look more like it is in heaven, and we get to be the conduits through which heaven touches earth and people are blessed. Learn as a MC to ask God where he's inviting you to join him in making the world a better place, and then take a risk and jump in. **Anything worth doing is worth doing poorly so you can get better!**

It can be tempting to think we have to be feeding the homeless or eradicating poverty in our city to have a legitimate OUT expression. **Little things matter in the kingdom, and your MC will find it easier to get involved if you start with something lightweight and low-maintenance.** Small things done over and over lead to big changes.

Leaning on the OUT of others: I have coached many MCs who struggled to develop a robust OUT expression and believed they were failures. Failure is only an unwillingness to learn and grow. The truth is this is easier for some than others, depending on the personalities, giftings, and training of the MC leaders. Here are a few encouragements for those who may struggle to develop their OUT dimension.

Lean on the OUT of others. In other words, find out who is doing OUT well and see if you can learn from them or be inspired by them.

Maybe your Church or other local non-profits have OUT opportunities your MC can join in on. Don't feel you have to reinvent the wheel of mission. Join others when helpful. I have even seen MCs become the missional force in many churches as they took ownership for missional initiatives previously run by staff!

Often MC leaders believe they have to have all the vision for their MC. Take time to invite the members of your MC if they see any OUT opportunities the whole group can join in on. Learn to lean on all the resources available within your MC.

In many cases MCs will begin with a clearly defined OUT expression that will be part of what draws others into the MC, but it can take time to develop a predictable and sustainable OUT dimension. Be patient. Keep learning. That's the goal.

Notes

Notes

Leading a MC

The most challenging paradigm shift for leaders of MCs is moving from a corporate metaphor, where we see ourselves as managers and facilitators, to the primary Biblical metaphor of family, where we see ourselves as spiritual parents, responsible for leading and maturing those entrusted to our care. This family metaphor is more fully developed in *Family on Mission*[6] but outlined here with some added texture for the MC context. The following is a helpful lens as you learn to lead into the UP, IN, and OUT lifestyle with the right perspective—*as a family*!

UP — Spiritual Parenting: *Taking responsibility for the family*

Every family needs parents. Parents provide direction, clarity, and confidence as the members of the family both learn their place in the family and how to represent the family well. We do not use this term so we can patronize those we lead but to help the leaders of MC better understand the nature of their responsibility.

Empowering: Spiritual Parents/Leaders (we use these terms interchangeably) are not overpowering, but empowering. Good leaders desire that those they lead would go farther than they themselves have gone. All good parents expect their ceiling will become their children's floor, and so every good MC leader invests in their MC to empower them as the priesthood of believers hoping that many of their "children" will one day help lead their own family. The leader's

---

[6] FOM, Mike and Sally Breen

job is not only to lead the family, but also to train the members of the family to take greater responsibility within the family and even to see some of those members start new families eventually.

As leaders we must begin with where people are, not where we wish they were. Don't be afraid to empower the more mature members of your MC and make room for them to express their strengths. This is what good parents do with their kids.

Spiritual Parents/Leaders help to set culture of the family, which is defined both by the language the family uses and the predictable patterns they practice. A major responsibility of the leaders of a MC is to define these and maintain consistency. We have to be careful not to take a legalistic approach, but a discipling/growth approach.

Spiritual parenting is NOT an age, gender, or even married issue (Jesus was single!). Spiritual leadership is about inviting others to join you in your family rhythms (whatever they look like) and taking responsibility for how they integrate into and function as part of the growing family.

I think parenting is one of the scariest responsibilities anyone can assume. I find I make more mistakes and failures than is fair for my own children, but the Lord continues to remind me that as I humbly commit to growing, so will those in our MC.

Spiritual parenting is simple, but very hard. (I'm convinced that children are the cause of grey hair!) Here are a few encouragements to remember when the road gets difficult:

It's hard, but worth it! Leading a family is really challenging, but we continue trying because the rewards are worth the sacrifice.

No one begins as a perfect parent. No matter how many books you read, seminars you attend, or how amazing your own parents were, it only takes a few hours, days, or months to realize that parenting is really challenging and that you're going to make lots of mistakes. Let those failures and struggles become the stepping stones to growth and learning, not stumbling blocks to progress.

Most of parenting is on-the-job training!

IN — Predictable Patterns: *Investing for fruitfulness*

Predictable patterns are the simple rhythms your family practices when you gather. We have offered imitatable patterns we believe are worth starting with in the section on UP-IN and IN-OUT Rhythms. Remember, we've given you a helpful starting point, but over time you will begin to modify your patterns to better fit your family.

Don't underestimate the value of doing the same things over and over again. We can fall prey in our entertainment culture to trying to create a whole new experience every MC gathering. Healthy families are the byproduct of healthy disciplines and patterns of engagement. **Healthy disciplines lead to healthy rhythms which produce healthy fruit.**

Attention Pioneers: There will always be the tension to feel like you want to change things up, do something different, add a little extra bit, etc. It may be that you cringe when you think of doing the same thing AGAIN and AGAIN and AGAIN, but that probably means you should continue with it! We shape culture by doing the same things over and over until it's just what we do. This is what creates lifestyle.

We all have predictable patterns in our lives, like the time we wake up each morning, what we eat for breakfast, wear to work or school, how we brush our teeth or wash our hair, the route we drive to work, what and when you eat, etc. The question is whether those patterns produce the fruit you're looking for. If not, then find some that do. Don't be afraid to try things out for a season and recalibrate later for greater fruitfulness. **Remember, we have to imitate before we innovate so find people who have more effective patterns and copy them.**

The reason we provide the MC Framework in the next section is because we know the importance of having some simple tracks to run on, disciplines that we have seen over many different MC experiences produce lots of incredible fruit. Are these the only disciplines? No, but we know the value of providing something you can imitate until you are ready to innovate.

OUT — Missional Purpose: A missional lifestyle is a choice, not a preference

The missional life is about learning to walk in the wake of God's grace. More often than not, OUT is the most intimidating aspect for many MCs, but remember, anything worth doing is worth doing poorly.

Some helpful reminders when leading your MC into the OUT dimension:

> *Trying is succeeding:* Create a culture of growth and experimentation by inviting people to try things and debrief them afterward to see what you can learn.

> *Setting the bar:* Set the bar according to where your people are, not just where you as the leader are. Remember, you're trying to help them grow. You wouldn't expect your 4-year-old to do the same things as your 16-year-old.

Don't use guilt, but invite and encourage your people into OUT opportunities. We've organized OUT activities for our MCs where only a few showed up. It is tempting to chastise your people or give up on them, but often they just need continued encouragement and over time you will see more of them stepping out.

Celebrate every little step! Celebrate what you want people to do more.

Lead the way: As with our own children, we have to lead the way in living the values and practices we want our children to grow in, until those values become their values. **Lead the way and hold the line (graciously) until you find that others are beginning to hold the line with you. _Those are your disciples!_**

Debrief, debrief, debrief: Make sure to create some time to debrief the OUT experiences you have with your MC. They need space to reflect, ask questions, and receive helpful coaching.

More Helpful Tips for Leading a MC

Invitation and Challenge[7]:

The way God helps us grow is by inviting us more deeply into his Covenant family so that we might learn to enjoy all the benefits of being part of his household. He also challenges us to grow up and increase in our maturity by taking on more responsibility, so we can represent his will and ways more effectively in every area of our lives. It is important to calibrate invitation and challenge to help the members of your MC grow.

---

[7] Invitation & Challenge, BDC, Breen

Some reflections on calibrating Invitation and Challenge:

The only way to help people grow is to help them identify where God is seeking to grow them (challenge) and to encourage, equip, and pray with them (invitation) as they make space for God to transform them.

You are already calibrating loads of invitation by inviting people into your lives, your home, by praying for them, encouraging them, feeding them and sharing with them. So don't be afraid to also share your expectations of them.

You will want to calibrate invitation and challenge based on the level of responsibility a person is carrying. Core team members should receive greater invitation and challenge than newcomers.

It is good to remember that the culture will reflect the strengths and weaknesses of the leadership, so pay attention to whether you lean more naturally to invitation or challenge and to make sure your MC does not become dominated by one or the other.

Special notes on bringing challenge in a MC:

Challenge should always come in the form of an invitation into the more that God has for someone.

Bring challenge where people are not reflecting the agreed values and practices of your MC.

Bring challenge only with those you are prepared to walk with as they grow. If we're not careful, we can become overpowering rather than empowering.

Helping people within your MC grow will require times where you bring challenge to individuals and/or the group as a whole. **When in doubt follow a wise rule: affirm publicly and correct privately.**

MC is not the place where we fix people. MC is the place where people are safe to see where God wants to grow them and where they have a community of people who are committed to helping them engage God for their growth.

You will soon realize that the greatest challenge in the MC lifestyle is not necessarily the mission, but the brokenness, dysfunctions, and immaturities exposed in the lives and families of those who are part of the MC. This is family, and family can be messy, but it's worth it. **As you are willing to engage in the brokenness of your MC family, you will receive greater grace and strength to reach those outside of your MC.**

Building family takes time (Trusting the process)

No one goes to the gym once expecting to see amazing results (unless they're delusional). Fitness requires a commitment to a healthy, regular, disciplined, intentional regimen, knowing results take time to reveal themselves. Trust the process!

Instead of assessing your MC every week, commit yourselves to a simple pattern of gathering and only assessing the health and fruitfulness of your MC in 3-6 month stages. **(For more on assessing your MC, see the section on Knowing if you're Winning.)**

Don't overreact: Human beings are creatures of overreaction. You will be tempted with every question, concern, or new idea to yank the steering wheel in a new direction. In the same way that you can't afford to lead your own household this way, don't lead your MC this way.

Feel free to receive any and all questions, reflections, and criticisms of the MC, but let those people know that you will take them to your team and the Lord for consideration but cannot guarantee any immediate changes. There is at least a sliver of truth in every criticism. So be open to what others say even when it is shared unhealthily. Mine out what truth there is and discard the rest.

Support and accountability

We don't recommend leading a MC unless YOU have support and accountability. God intended from the beginning that children would learn how to parent/lead from those who have gone before them and those who are also on the journey. Make sure you have some person(s) that can provide the support and accountability you will certainly need as you seek to lead an extended family on mission. The MCs we have led always benefitted when we had ongoing mentorship.

Leaders create culture

You will lead out of who you are. Leaders shape culture, and because we are all created with different personalities, gift mixes, and develop different skills, our MCs will reflect who we are for better and worse. Understanding who we are and how we're wired will be helpful so we can celebrate our strengths and grow in our weaknesses. Here are some helpful tools and reflections to help you toward greater self awareness and leadership:

> **Fivefold ministry:** We believe every person is wired to emphasize one of the fivefold ministries over the others (i.e. Apostle, Prophet, Evangelist, Pastor, Teacher) which will affect how your MC develops. We recommend you engage the Fivefold Ministry conversation found in BDC[8] and utilize

---

[8] Pentagon, BDC, Breen

---

the Fivefold Ministry Assessment to better understand yourself and your team. *(Visit http://fivefoldsurvey.com/ for a free online test available in English or Spanish.)*

Introvert vs. extrovert: While introverts will be tempted to protect their homes, families, and their time in leading a MC, extroverts will be tempted to pass over their families' needs and healthy boundaries in order to accommodate everyone in the MC. It is tempting to think a good MC leader will open their home and life 24/7 to any who would enter. This is not the case. It's important to be aware of your personality preferences, set healthy boundaries for your family/home, and have the support and accountability to grow in both.

Pioneer vs. developer: Some folks are hardwired to try new things and look for fresh opportunities (pioneers), while others are wired to build what they currently have and strengthen their current context (developers). Both are incredibly important in any family. Our job as leaders is to pay attention to what God is saying to us and where he's leading us, and to trust him to sustain us and grow us as we lead into things that are comfortable for us and areas that are challenging for us.

From mechanical to lifestyle

The greatest challenge for MCs is moving from mechanical to lifestyle. **The first few months of a MC can feel a bit clunky since everyone is learning a new way of operating, but that's the way it should be. It takes time!** We must be committed to a simple, repeatable way of gathering and functioning for a season before people start to feel like it's a lifestyle. Few things we do are natural at first, but repetition makes it natural. Remember, culture is created when we do the same things over and over ad nausea until it just becomes the way we do things.

It will take 3-6 months before people begin to feel like MC life is normal life. This may differ based on the group you begin with and how often you meet, but it still stands as a helpful rule of thumb

Practice makes better

Most of us would prefer to be good at something without having to work at it, especially when our learning comes at the cost of making lots of mistakes at other's expense. Thankfully there is tool that can help us understand the journey toward becoming a better MC leader.

> **Unconscious Incompetence:** The journey begins by choosing to do something you've never done before, namely start and lead a MC. You may feel excited, nervous, uncertain, but usually your fears are outweighed by your faith. Have fun, go after it.

> **Conscious Incompetence:** Soon enough you'll begin to realize there's more to learn than you currently know. Faced with your incompetence you'll have some options:
> 1 Wallow in your incompetence
>
> 2) Pretend everything is OK and ignore the areas of your leadership and your MC that need to grow
>
> 3) Embrace your incompetencies as opportunity for growth and make room for God to grow you and your MC.

A few hints for leaders in this stage:

> You don't know what you don't know until you make room for others to help you see your blindspots.

We only get better by failing and learning (like how kids learn to walk). Real failure is choosing not to learn from your failures.

During this season you will be tempted to fix your MC or try lots of new things to make it better. For this reason, during this time stick to imitating the simple patterns we have offered in this guide or what you have received from your leadership.

Conscious Competence: Your confidence is growing. You're getting a handle on it. You know more than you did when you started the journey, and the focus in this season is simply practicing the things you're learning. Practice makes better. This is also the stage where you will want to be increasingly intentional about training others to do what you've been learning to do. Nothing cements what you've learned like training others in what you've learned!

Unconscious Competence: At this stage you lead your MC without having to give it a ton of thought. You feel comfortable, you're training others, and your role will become more of a mentor to those you've been training. This is likely the stage where you will want to be thinking about multiplying your MC.

Notes

_____

_____

_____

_____

_____

_____

Notes

Practicalities of MC Life

Home size

I've never been in a home that is too small to host a MC. We've seen incredible MCs develop in small apartments, condos, townhomes, duplexes, in the inner city, suburbs, and in rural areas. The space may limit how many people you can fit, but we have found that is usually a good thing, not a bad thing. Remember, people don't feel like family until they have to get their own cup or plate, take out your trash, sit on the floor while they eat, clean up from a spill on your couch, or help clean marker off the wall.

You may outgrow your home, but that might mean you need to multiply, not get a bigger home!

Be careful not to fall into the trap of thinking your home has to be *Home and Garden* ready for MC gatherings. We will pick up around our home before people show up or ask our core team (those whom we are discipling) to come early to help us with that. We have to be careful not to let hosting a MC become too high maintenance—otherwise you will burn out quickly.

We understand that different cultures have different standards when it comes to hosting home gatherings. Whatever your culture, it will be very difficult to sustain an MC unless you learn how to make hosting it lightweight and low maintenance. ***If you can't imagine doing doing/hosting MC every week, then it's probably too high maintenance!***

Geography

The location of the host home matters, but not nearly as much as most think. Sometimes those who want to do MC together may be 30+ minutes away from one another. We may be scattered across a large geographic area. This is especially true in suburban and rural areas. Just remember that you may drive further for work or for the kid's sports practices. The question is rarely really about geography, but more about priorities.

We do think it can be fun to rotate homes after you have been gathering for 3+ months, but a consistent place is best in the early days to create predictable rhythms. If you rotate homes, it can be difficult for those who don't come for every gathering to know where the next gathering will occur.

Meeting times

We all have 24 hours in a day and 7 days in a week, and have to make tons of choices about how we will prioritize the investment of our time, energy, and resources. Every person/family will have to make a decision whether they will make the necessary adjustments to be part of the MC. I've never met anyone too busy for MC, but I have met many who decide not to prioritize it. This is a choice and requires sacrifice no matter how you look at it.

We have frequently had to make a choice for our children not to participate in youth sports on our MC night or to sacrifice Friday or Saturday nights in order to make a MC gathering work. If what you believe you will get out of the MC in the long run isn't worth the sacrifice, then you will likely find any reason not to make it happen. We have lamented at times when our closest friends weren't able to participate in our MC because they had a different commitment/priority or chose a different MC.

We usually do our best to make sure our core team is available on the MC night, but if you wait around until everyone's schedules work, you may find you never start the MC.

How often should we meet?

We strongly recommend a weekly MC gathering for the first 6-9 months as a way of establishing the rhythms of this new lifestyle. Remember, simple disciplines practiced repeatedly are what produce healthy rhythms and fruit. Therefore the more consistent, predictable, and regular your MC gatherings, the more easily it will become a lifestyle for your group.

Once MC is just a part of how you live, then you can explore other rhythms. Some MCs have moved to bi-weekly (every other week), while others move to three times per month and others remain weekly. We do not recommend moving to less than every other week if you intend for the community to grow well together

Communicating with our MC

We have made use of various social media platforms (Facebook, GroupMe, etc.) to communicate and keep our MC up to speed and on the same page. Utilize the technology to communicate things like:

Meal plans
Prayer requests, updates, and reminders
OUT activities, instructions and directions
Pictures from our gatherings
Plans for Parties
Funny videos

Numbers and Attendance — WHO vs. HOW MANY

You will be tempted to judge the success of your MC gatherings based on how many people show up each week. Numbers matter, but not for the reasons we often think.

Choose the right counting: In our home we count the number of people that show up to our dinner table for a few reasons: are all those currently living with us present? How many guests do we have with us for that particular meal? What are the needs related to the number of people present? These are practical realities. We need to be aware of who has shown up to our MC, but not because more is necessarily better. Focus on the WHO over the HOW MANY. As your MC looks more and more like Jesus' MC, God will add to your number. **Put your focus on who's there, not on who's not there.**

Avoid bad thinking: Because of the feudalistic mindset that has crept into the church world, the two things we count are the number of people attending services and how much they tithe. Poor church staffs will be depressed all week if they receive a poor report on either, and yet may have no idea what those numbers actually represent. Pressures to grow a church can drive staff to focus on good things in a bad way. Staff meetings are often dominated by that time where everyone reports on the numbers for their respective ministries. This mindset can creep into everything the church does and rob us of the freedom and joy of celebrating process, growth, and fruitfulness.

We have found without exception that, as we focused on getting more people to our MCs, they plateaued or shrank. When we focused on growing our people, our MCs grew and even multiplied!

We recommend having a core group of people in your MC (4-8 people) who are committed to consistent presence, while others will come and go as they can for various reasons. You will find over time that many will increase their consistency as they experience the benefits of the MC.

> **The core group:** The culture of any MC will be established not by those who come infrequently, but by the core group who are committed to regular presence and participation. These are those who own the responsibility of helping to lead the family and primarily by their example. Remember, people will do more of what you do than what you say.

> **Fringe:** There will be and should be folks who for many reasons cannot come regularly. Perhaps they are not yet Christians but are still drawn to come occasionally, or committed Christians whose schedules are shifting or difficult to align with your gathering times. Be OK with these fringe folks. Make room for them and be gracious to them. Many of these fringe folks have over time grown to become core in our MCs, and some have even gone on to lead their own MCs!

You will need to discern when and how to calibrate invitation and challenge[9] with individuals and families to help them grow in what God is seeking to grow them in. One person will need to commit to regular participation, while another will need grace for how seasonal circumstances keep them from being regular. Like Jesus, we need to be more interested in what God is doing in their lives than in making sure we feel good about how many showed up to MC.

---

[9] BDC, Breen

MCs are seasonal

MCs are not meant to last forever. We start MCs with the hope that they will grow and multiply, but we also have to be aware that people move, circumstances shift, life happens. Therefore, we recommend you think of MCs as seasonal. That season may be one year or five. Your MC may multiply many times or may never multiply. You may lead one that goes on for years and the next one you start lasts only one year.

Many factors affect the duration of a MC. Some of those might be:

How long the Lord calls the leaders to lead it: There may be other leaders who are ready and called to step up and continue the MC or not. Too often we can get stuck thinking that everything we start must continue forever and can easily pass over what God is doing in favor of what we prefer. Because MCs are the training wheels for **oikos** (healthy extended family relationships), even if the formal aspects of the MC cease, the relationships don't.

The MC fizzles out or never really gets going: This happens. Don't stress over it, but learn from it. What are the reasons the group may have fizzled?

Was it a leadership issue?

Was there not enough OUT to grow the group?

Were you too challenging or not challenging enough?

Were you meeting at an unrealistic time during the week?

Did people feel empowered?

Did you foster a sense of family or was it just another church activity that people checked off on their list?

MCs may come and go, but the relationships that are birthed and nurtured within the MC may last the rest of your life. Today we still enjoy many incredible relationships that were born out of the many MCs we have led and been part of in many different cities across the US over the past 13 years.

We plant and water, but God causes the growth. Some MCs, no matter what you invest into them and their leadership, just will not grow in that season. We've worked with plenty of leaders who floundered in their early attempts to lead a MC only to find that by their second, third, or even fourth attempts they were leading a flourishing MC that really became a powerful expression of God's Family on Mission.

Finances: Should we be tithing to our MC?

We recommend that MC participants continue tithing to their local churches and other support/investment opportunities as the Lord leads.

We highly recommend that the finances required to function as a MC come out of the overflow of the family and should be above and beyond the standard giving encouraged by churches. As MCs are not a church program, but rather an expression of everyday life, it is expected that the costs of being in a MC will be the responsibility of those who are part of the MC.

We have many times taken an offering within our MCs for various reasons like: purchasing supplies to paint a neighbor's fence, buying food for a family in need, helping to pay a plane ticket for someone to visit their dying family member, etc. Family helps family!

Kids: What do we do with our kids?

We have already included notes on what to do with kids in other sections, but here are a few more tips as you seek to incorporate all members of your growing family in a sustainable way. (Please note that we understand there are MCs that will not have kids, so do not feel pressured to find kids to be part of your MC if they are not already.)

You can't grow as a family without the kids. As you can probably tell, we have a high value for integrating kids into all we do. We believe the reason why so many young adults and families that have grown up in the church aren't coming back is because for most of their upbringing they were separated into their own programs, activities and generally treated like they had very little if anything to offer the rest of the family of God (except for the occasional Christmas show). As they mature they will eventually go where someone will take them seriously.

Take your kids seriously! Your kids are capable of hearing and responding to God's voice, praying for healing, sharing from God's word, etc. We have too often considered these adult activities and therefore have lost in many cases the benefits of what God has for us because of an unfortunate prejudice we unknowingly developed. Of course they will need training and lots of grace as they stumble, bumble, and fumble to find their way. But let's be honest—so do we.

As in any family activities, there are times when particular discussions or activities are not kid-appropriate, and in those cases you'll have to make a decision whether it's best to remove the kids or to rethink your activity.

Kids are not an interruption, but they can be a distraction. It can be difficult to know the line between kids just letting off energy and when they have crossed a line. The leaders of the MC will have to set those boundaries and enforce them.

Here are some ideas for when children become unruly, too loud, disruptive or show signs of a lack of healthy discipline:

Tell them again, again and again: Kids have a short memory, so you'll have to remind them over and over about the values and boundaries of how the family operates. We use the phrase, "Remember, this is how we _____." This emphasizes that we're all in it together and enforces the family's values for everyone, not just for kids.

Parents are ultimately responsible for their kids, even though it takes a village to raise a child. Sometimes you will need to speak to parents about their children's behavior as they may need to be discipled in an area of parenting. We recommend you do this in private to avoid embarrassing the parents.

Remember, a MC is the coming together of many different people representing different upbringings, disciplinary tactics and values. You'll have to patiently persevere by holding the line and graciously making room for others to adjust to your MC family values.

Babies: We always remind parents they can leave the room at any time with a fussy baby, but that we would rather the baby be a bit of a distraction and have mom/dad present than the parents leaving all the time for fear of being a distraction.

Be careful when you bring any kind of discipline to other people's children. All parents have their own way of handling their children, and you will want to emphasize that any gentle corrections given by the leaders are meant to help kids function within this family context, even if the rules are different at home.

Our rule has been, when in doubt, figure out how to include the kids. They will change how you sing, what thanksgivings sounds like, the nature of the family devotions, and the way your MC engages OUT opportunities. But this is discipleship, this is family. We cannot afford to outsource the discipleship of our children. Instead we need to live in such a way that we make space for them to learn, grow, and contribute without patronizing them or handling them in a disempowering manner.

In our experience our children have led us in openness, vulnerability, fun, lightheartedness, and faith. Many physical healings have come at the hands of our children's prayers. They have shared powerful and significant prophetic pictures and insights (often not even realizing how insightful). They have a simple, genuine faith that allows them to ask for the things that we as adults have become too civilized to ask God for. Much has been lost in the Christian community on account of not knowing how to include our children.

Who should we be inviting to our MC?

It is really important that you do not bait and switch people. In other words, be very upfront and honest about any kind of MC gathering to which you may invite others. We encourage you to think of the different gatherings of your MC like concentric circles, with each circle inward representing a greater degree of open spiritual engagement. These circles are described from the innermost to the outermost.

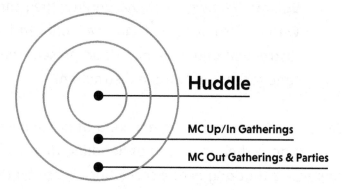

Huddle

MC Up/In Gatherings

MC Out Gatherings & Parties

Huddle: This gathering is obviously for those who have been part of the extended family and are POPs—those you feel called to disciple with the hope they will lead a MC in the future. This is the highest bar of spiritual investment, and you only want to invite those who you believe are ready for this opportunity. These are often part of your core team that help you start the MC.

MC (UP-IN Gatherings): These are meant to be openly spiritual and reflect the basic predictable patterns that will help the growing family to engage with God and one another. You can invite people who are not yet Christians, but you want to make sure you give them a heads up about what they will step into.

MC (IN-OUT Activities): Interestingly, we have found people who are not yet Christians are often very interested in joining us as we serve our local community. However, we are still very open about what we'll be doing and spiritual activities that we may engage in while practicing the OUT dimension. There is little about your community that will be more compelling than a group of people who enjoy being together and for whom their spirituality is just a natural part and overflow of their lives, not an add on.

Parties and other fun activities: These are great contexts to invite anyone and everyone into! We encourage our MC to look for every opportunity to invite neighbors, family members, coworkers, etc, to any of these activities. We promise not to treat their friends like targets. Pay attention to what God is doing and who he may be nudging you to invite. God will surprise you.

Notes

How to Start a MC
Laying a Firm Foundation

Select your team

It's ideal to start a MC with a core team of people (6-8) who are committed to learning and leading as representatives of the extended family (MC). This core team will serve as the nucleus as others begin to orbit in.

Your core team should be POPs to you. They like you, welcome your leadership investment, and seek to serve your mission.

Spend some time with your core team reading through the introduction of this MC Leader Guide before starting your MC Rhythms. This will build helpful unity around core values of how you will operate. This will also give you an opportunity to begin assessing a possible Mission Vision as well as processing together who you may invite to participate in this MC.

Disciple your team (Huddle)

We're assuming the person utilizing this leader guide has a working knowledge and practice with the core 3DM tools for building a discipling culture. We believe that, under the hood of every MC, there must be a discipleship engine. If you do not have leaders in your midst who can serve you in this way, we recommend connecting with one of our certified 3DM Coaches who can help you learn how to build a discipling culture.

Whatever tools you use, please make sure you are committed to training people within your MC who can eventually start their own MCs. The kingdom of God is reproductive and grows, and so we must lead families with the intention of multiplying more families. This requires a discipleship/reproductive culture.

Train your team in the character and competencies expected of those who are functioning maturely within the extended family unit. These core people should be functioning as the older siblings of the MC. They bear greater responsibility but also receive a greater investment.

Train your team

We have found it very helpful to gather as an MC with just your core team for a month or two in the beginning in order to establish how the MC will function before inviting others into it. You may want to go through the first 2-3 months of the framework offered in the next section before inviting others. This gives you an opportunity to coach, train, and process how the MC will function before inviting others into the mix. This doesn't mean you won't recalibrate along the way, but having a core group that is all on the same page is very helpful in creating the culture.

Make sure your core team understands the biblical basis for why and what you do what you do together. For help with this, we recommend reading LMC and FOM.[10]

Give the core team members clear expectations for how they should function within the MC context. What roles do you expect them to fulfill? How should they be investing in those who begin to join the MC?

If you want to create a culture of vulnerability, then the core team goes first.

---

[10] LMC & FOM, Breen

Praying out loud? The core team goes first. Healing prayer? The core team goes first. Experimentation in mission? The core team goes first. Inviting POPs to parties? The core team goes first. You get the picture.

Can we start a MC without a Core Group?

This is the classic Chicken or Egg dilemma. In our collective experience of starting MCs, we have found that sometimes this is necessary. Let me explain: Sometimes we have found ourselves in contexts where there are not many with significant Christian maturity and therefore, in order to find our disciples, we gathered first with those who seemed to be drawn to us (MC) and over time were able to discern those who were ready to grow more significantly (Huddle).

This is often how we coach church planters to start who have moved to a new area without a team. (I'm referring here to parachute drops.)

Interestingly, Jesus started his public ministry and even joined the **oikos**/ extended family of Peter and Andrew before he called his first disciples. We generally recommend starting a MC with a core team. Starting a MC without a core team requires a high level of apostolic energy and is far more difficult in our experience—not impossible, but more difficult.

Transitioning preexisting groups into MCs

Can we transition a Small group, Life Group, etc to a MC? Yes! You can transition any group to a MC. However here are some important things to consider when doing so:

> The most important persons to consider for this kind of transition are the leaders. If the leaders catch the vision for the MC life (UP, IN, OUT) and are committed to leading their current group into this new way of operating, then there's a good chance they will succeed. These leaders will need ongoing support and accountability for this journey.

> Whether you are transitioning a small group, life group, or any other group toward the MC lifestyle, you will want to make sure you are upfront and clear with the group about the transition. Give them an opportunity to process, pray, and ask lots of questions before making any shift. Otherwise the group will likely feel caught off guard and resistant. This will require that you, as the leader, have clarity about the what and why of the changes.

> If your group is associated with a church, then it is best if you confirm with your leaders any shifts you may seek to make before attempting them.

Culture shifts: Remember, shifting to the MC life is introducing new cultural dimensions that may prove challenging for the current group. No matter how you slice it, change can be very difficult. It requires patience, grace, empathy, and perseverance. You will have to remind your group of the why over and over again.

Don't throw the baby out with the bathwater! It can be very tempting (especially for pioneering leaders) to accidentally discard all you have been doing in favor of the new thing. We encourage you to preserve as much of the way you have been operating and celebrate it as you begin to introduce bit by bit the new ideas.

Starting MCs in a Church Setting

No matter how tempting it can be, we don't recommend letting people sign up for your MC as a response to a Sunday morning service/sermon. This is how you start programs, not grow families.

MCs grow better by word of mouth and the attractive lives and relationships of those in the MC. If no one is attracted to your MC, and the people in your MC don't ever have anyone they can bring into these relationships, then that's the place to begin working.

We do highly recommend letting people in your church know there are MCs gathering and giving people the contact info for the leadership of the MCs so that those who are interested can inquire.

Testimony, Testimony, Testimony: Share lots of testimonies from the great things happening in your MCs during your weekend services as this will build interest. We recommend having someone from the MC share the testimony in order to give a face to the MC.

We encourage church staffs to train their MC leaders and teams to see every church event as fishing ponds from which they are luring new folks into their MC. Everyone is fair game!

Notes

Assessing, Growing
& Reproducing your MC

Knowing if you're Winning — MC Assessment

It is important to have a way of measuring growth. How do we know if we are winning in what we are doing? Below are sets of reflective questions that will help you perform diagnostics on your MC to evaluate growth and traction. We use the three dimensions of the FOM triangle to keep it simple.

We recommend reflecting on these questions as a leadership team every 2-3 months. Which questions most stand out to you? Take time to process those particular questions and see what God is saying to you? Invite others with more experience or leaders in your church to help you discern the best way of making recalibrations.

Spiritual parenting:

Do you have clear leadership?

Are those leaders taking responsibility for leading the MC in the simple UP/IN and IN/OUT rhythms?

Are the vision and values of the MC simple, clear, and articulated?

Are the leaders providing a balance of invitation and challenge to help the MC members grow?

Are the leaders providing opportunities for others to take on more responsibility in the family functions?

Use the Hexagon[11] to evaluate the UP dimension of your MC.

Use the Heptagon[12] to evaluate the IN dimension of your MC.

Use the Octagon[13] to evaluate the OUT dimension of your MC.

Predictable patterns

Has your MC moved from mechanical to natural in the UP/IN rhythms?

Are your gatherings consistent enough that your people can predict what you're doing each time?

Are more people sharing more freely during times of thanksgiving?

Are people more comfortable praying for each other?

Are you getting to know the stories of the various members of your MC?

Are people lingering longer after the official ending time of your MC?

Are your people inviting others to join in your MC gatherings?

---

[11] BDC, Hexagon. Breen

[12] BDC, Heptagon. Breen

[13] BDC, Octagon. Breen

Are people taking more initiative for the various responsibilities of your MC gatherings (i.e. bringing food, set up, clean up, taking the trash out, helping with the kids)?

Do your people seem more relaxed and comfortable during MC gatherings?

Are your people caring for one another?

Missional purpose

Do you have a clear Mission Vision for this season of your MC?

Are you leveraging the various members of your MC to discern your Mission Vision?

Are your MC members participating in your Mission Vision activities?

Are you keeping your missional activities lightweight and low maintenance?

Are you excluding MC members by the nature of your missional activities (kids, elderly, etc.)?

Are you throwing parties, and are your MC members inviting their friends?

Would anyone outside of your MC feel the loss if your MC ceased to exist?

Are you willing to experiment with different OUT activities to find what is best for this particular season?

Expanding your circles

There are different ways to grow your MC, but we offer here the simplest process that we find works for the greatest number of leaders. We call it expanding your circles. Think of your growing MC as a series of concentric circles where the innermost circle represents the greatest level of commitment and intimacy while the outermost circle represents the smallest level of commitment and intimacy. We encourage you to start by developing the innermost circle that will give you the strength of a nucleus that others can begin to orbit around. It is much easier to create culture when you have at least a handful of people who are committed to that culture already.

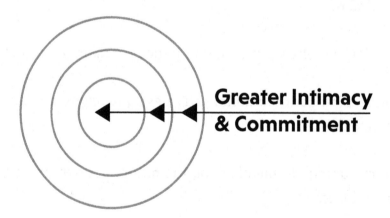

Greater Intimacy & Commitment

We have labeled each of the circles to give you an idea of how you can grow from the inner circles to the other circles. (Note: Many have noticed that Jesus seemed to call his disciples after he had already been operating within Peter and Andrew's *oikos*. I believe this may very well have been the case. However Jesus was functioning with a significantly greater degree of leadership capacity than most of us are beginning with, so we recommend starting with a team of disciples.)

If you have gathered for a short season with just your core team, make sure to be praying for POPs, and make sure to invite your POPs to an appropriate type of gathering. Some POPs should be invited into your UP/IN gatherings, while others should be invited first to one of your parties.

Reproducing MCs – Building the future

Life in the kingdom grows and multiplies: Families should grow and multiply (Gen. 1:26-28). No parents have children with the expectation that they'll live at home forever. We understand that, as our children grow and mature, eventually they will seek to develop a healthy sense of interdependence and even start their own family. We should enter into MC life with a similar expectation. Not everyone will start their own MC, but the desire for everyone should be that they are growing and stepping into greater responsibility within the family, and that they will reproduce their life in others (discipleship) with the hopes that some will eventually start their own MCs.

If you are discipling some within your MC, over time these will be the ones who have an opportunity to start new MCs.

How do I know whether there are people in our MC who should be encouraged to lead their own MC?

> They will have been POPs to you. They will have submitted themselves to the culture and practices of your leadership, even though they may have their own ideas of how to do things. **Good followership is always the forerunner to good leadership.**

> They are the people you trust to lead in your stead when you are not present.

Leaders are those who have followers. Are there people that are drawn to them? Perhaps they lead a huddle or growing small group within your MC.

Sometimes these kinds of people will come to you with a vision for a new MC, and other times you will have to encourage them to consider starting a new MC.

We don't add MCs; we multiply MCs. Resist starting new MCs just because there are folks who want to be in one. Instead, only multiply MCs when you have leaders who are ready to start new MCs.

Again, we strongly encourage MCs to multiply from existing MCs. Someone does have to start the first one, but from that point forward we think they are better multiplied.

Notes

Part 2

1-Year MC Framework

The following pages present one way to launch your MC.

While these are only guidelines, they show a healthy rhythm of UP/IN/OUT and some important topics to cover.

If you are launching a MC with a core group, you may choose to go through the first 8-12 weeks with that group, and then repeat it as your group grows. That will ensure everyone understands the culture and goals that will power the MC.

In the pages that follow, we'll go into more detail about each week and what you can do. We offer a week-by-week outline that includes a MC schedule along with helpful tips for leaders. These outlines reflect the same patterns unpacked in earlier sections.

How to Use this Framework

Summary — Each week offers an at a glance summary of the theme and topic for that week. We've even offered a visual diagram so you know whether it is an UP/IN or IN/OUT week. Remember, as the leaders of your MC, you'll need to decide each week whether what is offered is the best next engagement for your MC. You may choose to review what was addressed the prior gathering or perhaps you sense the Lord wanting your MC to attend to something entirely different than what's offered in the framework for a week. You're the leader so you get to make the choice.

Schedule — This is your space to take notes as you think ahead to the next MC gathering. You'll see that for all the UP/IN gatherings there is space for taking notes. Though we recommend consistency, you can use the notes space to jot down ideas for meals, or who may lead a particular section of the night, or how you want to engage the Family Devotion or Small Group, or who will lead or how you'll engage the singing/worship component.

Leader Tips — There isn't enough space to share all of the things we've learned over the years, but in this section we offer what we hope are some key tips for leading each MC week. You'll see that some of the Leader Tips repeat for particular weeks which is our way of reminding you that consistency is very important. These aren't mandates, but ideas of how to lead your MC well. Feel free to recalibrate or innovate where you think necessary. Most importantly, have fun and remember this is a learning journey, not a test.

MC Gathering Review — Debriefing is a very important part of leadership as it promotes active learning through a process of simple reflection. We encourage a time of reviewing each gathering, not so you can determine whether you succeeded or failed, but rather to glean from the Lord and your leaders how you can continue growing in your leadership of this spiritual family. We've already included in each review 2 questions to prompt helpful reflection, but feel free to expand upon these. Just remember the big win is paying attention to what God is up to and doing your best to respond.

MC FRAMEWORK AT-A-GLANCE
A BALANCED LIFE

Interval 1 — A Balanced Life

- **Week 1: UP/IN:**
  Family Devotion — We're UP, IN, OUT people
  (Principles of Jesus = early church = today)

- **Week 2: UP/IN:**
  SGs — Identifying & Praying for POPs

- **Week 3: UP/IN:**
  SG Questions

- **Week 4: IN/OUT:**
  Mission Vision adventure

Interval 2 — A Balanced Life

- **Week 1: UP/IN:**
  Family Devotion — Explaining our UP & IN rhythms

- **Week 2: UP/IN:**
  SGs — Praying for POPs

- **Week 3: UP/IN:**
  SGs

- **Week 4: IN/OUT:**
  Mission Vision adventure

Interval 3 — A Balanced Life

■ **Week 1: UP/IN:**
Family Devotion — Developing our IN & OUT rhythms
(What is our Missional Purpose?)

■ **Week 2: UP/IN:**
SGs — Praying for POPs

■ **Week 3: UP/IN:**
SG Questions (Groups of 3-4)

■ **Week 4: IN/OUT:**
Mission Vision adventure

MC Assessment Exercise

FINDING FRUITFULNESS

Interval 4 — Finding Fruitfulness

- **Week 1: UP/IN:**
  Family Devotion — Learning to work from rest
  (Genesis 1-3, creation story)

- **Week 2: UP/IN:**
  SGs — Do I have a healthy personal work/rest rhythm

- **Week 3: UP/IN:**
  SG Questions (Groups of 3-4)

- **Week 4: IN/OUT:**
  Party or OUT adventures

Interval 5 — Finding Fruitfulness

- **Week 1: UP/IN:**
  Family Devotion — Living by indirect effort:
  Abiding & Fruitfulness (John 15)

- **Week 2: UP/IN:**
  SGs — Do I take intentional time to abide each day?

- **Week 3: UP/IN:**
  SG Questions (Groups of 3-4)

- **Week 4: IN/OUT:**
  Party or OUT adventure

Invterval 6 — Finding Fruitfulness

- **Week 1: UP/IN:**
  Family Devotion — Even greater fruitfulness!
  (Value of pruning/John 15:2)

- **Week 2: UP/IN:**
  SGs — Where is God trying to prune me/family for greater fruitfulness?

- **Week 3: UP/IN:**
  SG Questions (Groups of 3-4)

- **Week 4: IN/OUT:**
  Party or OUT adventure

MC Assessment Exercise

THE EMPOWERED LIFE

Interval 7 — The Empowered Life

- **Week 1: UP/IN:**
  Family Devotion — The Empowered Life: Invitation & Challenge

- **Week 2: UP/IN:**
  SGs — Is God inviting me or challenging me?

- **Week 3: UP/IN:**
  SG Questions (Groups of 3-4)

- **Week 4: IN/OUT:**
  Party or OUT adventure

Interval 8 — The Empowered Life

- **Week 1: UP/IN:**
  Family Devotion — Empowering Others:
  Leading with Invitation & Challenge

- **Week 2: UP/IN:**
  SGs — What kind of culture am I creating around me?

- **Week 3: UP/IN:**
  SG Questions (Groups of 3-4)

- **Week 4: IN/OUT:**
  Party or OUT adventure

Interval 9 — The Empowered Life

- **Week 1: UP/IN:**
  Family Devotion — Being an Empowered Community:
  Family on Mission

- **Week 2: UP/IN:**
  SGs — Where am I being empowered?

- **Week 3: UP/IN:**
  SG Questions (Groups of 3-4)

- **Week 4: IN/OUT:**
  Party or OUT adventure

MC Assessment Exercise

ENGAGING GOD

Interval 10 — Engaging God

- **Week 1: UP/IN:**
  Praying like Jesus

- **Week 2: UP/IN:**
  SGs — Understanding Dad

- **Week 3: UP/IN:**
  SG Questions (Groups of 3-4)

- **Week 4: IN/OUT:**
  Party or OUT adventure

Interval 11 — Engaging God

- **Week 1: UP/IN:**
  Family Devotion — What is God saying and doing? (Part 1)

- **Week 2: UP/IN:**
  SGs — Prayer Filtering

- **Week 3: UP/IN:**
  SG Questions (Groups of 3-4)

- **Week 4: IN/OUT:**
  Party or OUT adventure

Interval 12 — Engaging God

■ **Week 1: UP/IN:**
Family Devotion — What is God saying and doing? (Part 2)

■ **Week 2: UP/IN:**
SGs — Where am I being empowered?

■ **Week 3: UP/IN:**
SG Questions (Groups of 3-4)

■ **Week 4: IN/OUT:**
Party or OUT adventure

MC Assessment Exercise

Week 1 Summary

☑ UP/IN Gathering
☑ Family Devotion — We're UP, IN, OUT people.

MC Schedule

■ Eat (30 minutes)

Eat (30 min)
_____
_____
_____
_____

■ Thanksgiving (15 minutes)

Thanksgiving (15 min)
_____
_____
_____
_____

■ Singing/Worship (15 minutes)

Worship (15 min)
_____
_____
_____
_____

■ Family Devotion (20 minutes)

● —Small Group (20 min) _____

_____

_____

_____

_____

■ Prayer (10 minutes)

● —Prayer (10 min) _____

_____

_____

_____

_____

Leader Tips

■ Eat
- You'll want to make sure you have established a regular meal plan for those joining you and that you communicate if you change it up.
- Our meal plan has generally been a potluck where everyone brings enough to feed 4 others.

■ Family Devotion — We're UP, IN, OUT people
- (15 minutes) Share a simple vision for your MC as an UP, IN, OUT community.
  - Jesus lived a three-dimensional life that reflected a regular, rhythmic investment in the UP dimension—his relationship with the Father and Holy Spirit; the IN dimension—his relationship with his faith family (both blood and non-blood relationships); and his OUT dimension—his desire to see other become part of God's family.
  - For a fuller explanation of the three-dimensional life, read the

chapter on the Balanced Life in BDC.[14]

- You can illustrate these three dimensions using the Triangle. This is a helpful visual aid that will help both old and young grasp the three-dimensional life.

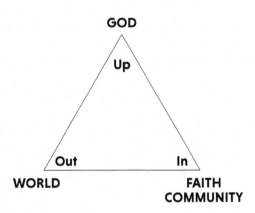

- Share a little about your journey growing in each dimension. Talk about both your successes and your struggles.
- Let them know your MC gatherings will help everyone to invest and grow in all three dimensions in different ways. This is something you can highlight as you go along from week to week.

- (5 minutes) Q & A. Invite your MC to share questions, reflections, etc. You will be processing the three dimensional life over the next few months so there's no hurry to solve every issue in this meeting.

---

[14] BDC, Breen

MC Gathering Review —

What went well? What would you do differently next time?

_____

_____

_____

_____

_____

_____

_____

_____

_____

_____

_____

_____

_____

_____

Interval 1 — A Balanced Life

Week 2 Summary

☑ UP/IN Gathering
☑ Small Groups — Identifying & Praying for POPs

MC Schedule

■ Eat (30 minutes)

Eat (30 min)

_____

_____

_____

_____

■ Thanksgiving (15 minutes)

Thanksgiving (15 min)

_____

_____

_____

_____

■ Singing/Worship (15 minutes)

Worship (15 min)

_____

_____

_____

_____

- **Small Groups (20 minutes)**

  ◗—Small Group (20 min) _____

  _____

  _____

  _____

- **Prayer (10 minutes)**

  ◗—Prayer (10 min) _____

  _____

  _____

  _____

Leader Tips

- Small Groups — Identifying & Praying for POP
  - (10 minutes) Introduce your MC to the POP strategy.
    - Jesus gives to his disciples the best strategy for reaching those who may not know God or who are estranged from him. He told his disciples to be on the lookout for people who are already showing signs that they are open to God and his people. Jesus called these Persons of Peace (POPs).[15]
    - We identify POPs by looking for those people who like us, who welcome us, and who seek to serve us.[16]
    - Share a little about your journey of learning to identify POPs. Share both the breakthroughs and battles.

---

[15] Luke 10:6

[16] Octagon, BDC, Breen.

- Remember, we have to be POPs to others before we can expect them to become POPs to us. God was first a POP to us before we became the same to him.

- (5 minutes) Invite everyone to take a few minutes to identify a few POPs in their life. Have them share these names with at least one person next to them.
- (5 minutes) Have everyone take time with one other person to pray for their POPs. Encourage them to keep it simple. They may just ask God to bless these persons.
- This activity helps your MC learn to identify people in whom God is already working, trains your MC to begin paying attention to what God is doing in others., and gives your MC folks to invite to IN/OUT activities.

MC Gathering Review –
What went well? What would you do differently next time?

_____

_____

_____

_____

_____

_____

_____

_____

_____

_____

_____

_____

_____

_____

_____

Week 3 Summary

- ☑ UP/IN Gathering
- ☑ Small Groups — SG Questions

MC Schedule

◼ Eat (30 minutes)

Eat (30 min)

_____

_____

_____

_____

◼ Thanksgiving (15 minutes)

Thanksgiving (15 min)

_____

_____

_____

_____

◼ Singing/Worship (15 minutes)

Worship (15 min)

_____

_____

_____

_____

■ Small Groups (20 minutes)

──────────────────────────────

Small Group (20 min) ────────────────────────

──────────────────────────────

──────────────────────────────

──────────────────────────────

──────────────────────────────

■ Prayer (10 minutes)

──────────────────────────────

Prayer (10 min) ──────────────────────────

──────────────────────────────

──────────────────────────────

──────────────────────────────

Leader Tips

■ Small Groups

- Use the Small Group Questions in the appendix. Make enough copies to share one sheet with each SG, and pass the sheets out as they go into SGs.
- We instruct members of our MC to get into groups of 3-4 and go through as many of the questions as they have time for.
- If you have a core team you are discipling and enough to divide the group, then have them raise their hands and let 2-3 others gather with them. They can be your SG leaders. You can encourage these leaders be consistent each time or allow people to gather spontaneously with a different group each time, depending on which seems to work better for your group

■ Debrief

- Leave 10 minutes at the end of your time together to regroup and share anything from SG that the rest of the family needs to know about. Maybe someone is celebrating a new job or has just found out they have a physical illness or are in need of a new job.

- We strongly encourage that people share for themselves and not for others. If they say they have permission to share for someone else, I always verify with that person on the spot first.
- We often take time to quickly pray for some of the things shared in this setting.

MC Gathering Review –

What went well? What would you do differently next time?

_____

_____

_____

_____

_____

_____

_____

_____

_____

_____

_____

_____

_____

_____

_____

Week 4 Summary

☑ IN/OUT Gathering
☑ OUT Adventure/Mission Vision

MC Schedule

■ You may choose to engage your OUT activity during the usual time of your UP/IN gatherings, or it may make more sense to do it on a different day of the week. During one season our MC met on Wednesday evenings, and our OUT activities were better engaged on the weekends, so that's what we did. On our IN/OUT weeks we have often moved our gathering time to the day/time that was most conducive to our OUT activity.

■ Of course, an OUT gathering your schedule will look different than your UP/IN gatherings. We recommend you gather together first to give clear instruction for the activity and also provide a few minutes on the back end to debrief your experience.
  ■ Gather for instruction.
  ■ Engage your Mission Vision (we discuss this fully in Part 1 under IN/OUT Rhythms).
  ■ Take a few minutes after the activity or at your next MC gathering to debrief the OUT experience with your MC.

Leader Tips

■ We offer lots of ideas in the Appendix that you can try and experiment with. You'll also want to make sure you are throwing a party at least once a month as well. This gives you a minimum of two OUT activities per month. You may do more, but two is a good starting point, especially for those for whom the OUT dimension is more challenging. Remember, predictable patterns like this will create a new culture in your heart and your MC.

■ Make sure to clearly communicate to your MC ahead of time what activity you will be engaging. Does the activity require special accessories like:
  - Walking shoes for a prayer walk
  - Paint brushes, rollers, etc for painting
  - Clean or dirty clothes
  - Games for a party

■ Be appreciative and empathetic with those who are uncomfortable about the OUT activity. Gently encourage them join you, even if they only watch or take a more passive or quiet role. You're helping everyone grow in the OUT dimension, but we have to begin where people are, not where we wish they were.

■ Be sensitive to the physical limitations for different OUT activities and consider whether you will be excluding members of your MC in an activity. Perhaps they can provide prayer support onsite or just a friendly smile to those you are serving.

Kids: Be sensitive to the ages of your MC's kids and how they can engage with your OUT activity

MC Gathering Review —

What went well? What would you do differently next time?

_____

_____

_____

_____

_____

_____

_____

_____

_____

_____

_____

_____

_____

_____

Week 1 Summary

☑ UP/IN Gathering
☑ Family Devotion — Explaining our UP/IN rhythms

MC Schedule

■ Eat (30 minutes)

_____
_____

_____

_____

_____

■ Thanksgiving (15 minutes)

_____

_____

_____

_____

■ Singing/Worship (15 minutes)

_____

_____

_____

_____

_____

- **Family Devotion (20 minutes)**

  Small Group (20 min) _____
  _____
  _____
  _____

- **Prayer (10 minutes)**

  Prayer (10 min) _____
  _____
  _____
  _____
  _____

Leader Tips

Thanksgiving: You will likely have to prod and encourage people to share, as this may be slightly uncomfortable for those who are newer to this experience. Also, the introverts will need time in silence to think—so you may want to offer a couple minutes at the outset before people start sharing. You can also remind your MC to come with thanksgivings prepared if they can. Again, you are creating a culture of thanksgiving by training your people in this way.

- Family Devotion — Explaining our UP/IN rhythms
  - (15 minutes) Explain how Jesus was rejected by his own family and friends in Luke 4:28-30, and then relocated to Capernaum and took up residence in Peter and Andrew's household. (*oikos*: the Greek word that means household and that describes the extended family, blood and non-blood relations, who would have lived together and worked together in most cases.) This became

home base for much of Jesus' ministry. They made room for Jesus in the daily rhythms of their **oikos**, and soon they began to reflect Jesus' rhythms of the three-dimensional life. Read the narrative from Luke 4:31-5:11 to see how this begins to unfold.

- Share the UP, IN, OUT Triangle and circle the UP & IN dimensions to show this first major rhythm of your MC. Unpack a bit about the predictable patterns of eating, thanksgiving, singing/worship, family devotions and small groups, and debrief/prayer. Let them know these reflect the healthy family patterns as revealed in Acts 2:42 and show them what those patterns produced in the community in 2:43-47.

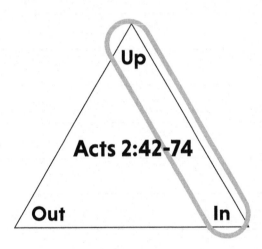

- Share a bit about the UP/IN rhythms you are developing in your own life and household. (These apply whether you are single or married).
- (5 minutes) Q & A

- Prayer — Finish your MC gathering by taking a few minutes to pray for any who are sick or who may stand in proxy for those who are sick.

MC Gathering Review –

What went well? What would you do differently next time?

_____

_____

_____

_____

_____

_____

_____

_____

_____

_____

_____

_____

_____

_____

_____

Week 2 Summary

☑ UP/IN Gathering
☑ Small Groups — Praying for POPs

MC Schedule

■ Eat (30 minutes)

Eat (30 min)

_____
_____
_____
_____

■ Thanksgiving (15 minutes)

Thanksgiving (15 min)

_____
_____
_____
_____

■ Singing/Worship (15 minutes)

Worship (15 min)

_____
_____
_____
_____

■ Small Groups (20 minutes)

Small Group (20 min) _____

_____

_____

_____

_____

■ Prayer (10 minutes)

Prayer (10 min) _____

_____

_____

_____

_____

Leader Tips

■ Eat — This will be a good week to offer encouragements to the MC regarding the food and meals. Some thoughts:

- Are people bringing food? Is the food they are bringing in line with the dietary needs of your MC? Is everyone bringing the same thing every week?
- We encourage singles to bring food also, even if it's a prepared meal bought from the store. In family, everyone contributes. We use to give the college kids an option to bring chips until we realized they all were bringing chips! Anyone can stop by the store and bring a rotisserie chicken, side of vegetables, or make a salad.
- Don't miss the opportunity to disciple your MC participants in this area. It's not about doing MC right, but about helping the family learn how to operate well together. Some will need help understanding what constitutes healthy food or the amount of

food that will actually serve the MC (we recommend enough to serve 4).

- Small Groups — Praying for POPs
  - Remind your MC about the POPs they have identified, and have them take time in their small groups to share about their POPs and pray for them. You can't spend too much time attending to POPs, as this will go far as you develop your OUT dimension as a MC.
  - Once you have given the MC clear instruction, send them into groups of 3-4.

Note:
Repeat the process of having the core team you are discipling volunteer to lead the small group time. Remember, it's OK to make these groups consistent, or to allow people to gather spontaneously with a different group each time. Find the rhythm that's right for your group

MC Gathering Review –

What went well? What would you do differently next time?

_____

_____

_____

_____

_____

_____

_____

_____

_____

_____

_____

_____

_____

_____

Week 3 Summary

☑ UP/IN Gathering
☑ Small Groups — SG Questions

MC Schedule

■ Eat (30 minutes)

Eat (30 min)

_____

_____

_____

_____

■ Thanksgiving (15 minutes)

Thanksgiving (15 min)

_____

_____

_____

_____

■ Singing/Worship (15 minutes)

Worship (15 min)

_____

_____

_____

_____

■ Small Groups (20 minutes)

Small Group (20 min) _____
_____
_____
_____
_____

■ Prayer (10 minutes)

Prayer (10 min) _____
_____
_____
_____
_____

Leader Tips

■ Small Groups
  ■ Use the Small Group Questions in the appendix. Make enough copies to share one sheet with each SG, and pass the sheets out as they go into SGs.
  ■ We instruct members of our MC to get into groups of 3-4 and go through as many of the questions as they have time for.
  ■ If you have a core team you are discipling and enough to divide the group, then have them raise their hands and let 2-3 others gather with them. They can be your SG leaders. You can encourage these leaders be consistent each time or allow people to gather spontaneously with a different group each time, depending on which seems to work better for your group.

■ Debrief
  ▪ Leave 10 minutes at the end of your time together to regroup and share anything from SG that the rest of the family needs to know about. Maybe someone is celebrating a new job or has just found out they have a physical illness or are in need of a new job.
  ▪ We strongly encourage that people share for themselves and not for others. If they say they have permission to share for someone else, I always verify with that person on the spot first.
  ▪ We often take time to quickly pray for some of the things shared in this setting.

MC Gathering Review –

What went well? What would you do differently next time?

_____

_____

_____

_____

_____

_____

_____

_____

_____

_____

_____

_____

_____

_____

_____

Week 4 Summary

☑ IN/OUT Gathering
☑ OUT Adventure/Mission Vision

MC Schedule

■ You may choose to engage your OUT activity during the usual time of your UP/IN gatherings, or it may make more sense to do it on a different day of the week. During one season our MC met on Wednesday evenings, and our OUT activities were better engaged on the weekends, so that's what we did. On our IN/OUT weeks we have often moved our gathering time to the day/time that was most conducive to our OUT activity.

■ Of course, an OUT gathering your schedule will look different than your UP/IN gatherings. We recommend you gather together first to give clear instruction for the activity and also provide a few minutes on the back end to debrief your experience.

   ▪ Gather for instruction.
   ▪ Engage your Mission Vision (we discuss this fully in Part 1 under IN/OUT Rhythms).
   ▪ Take a few minutes after the activity or at your next MC gathering to debrief the OUT experience with your MC.

Leader Tips

■ We offer lots of ideas in the Appendix that you can try and experiment with. You'll also want to make sure you are throwing a party at least once a month as well. This gives you a minimum of two OUT activities per month. You may do more, but two is a good starting point, especially for those for whom the OUT dimension is more challenging. Remember, predictable patterns like this will create a new culture in your heart and your MC.

■ Make sure to clearly communicate to your MC ahead of time what activity you will be engaging. Does the activity require special accessories like:
  - Walking shoes for a prayer walk
  - Paint brushes, rollers, etc for painting
  - Clean or dirty clothes
  - Games for a party

■ Be appreciative and empathetic with those who are uncomfortable about the OUT activity. Gently encourage them join you, even if they only watch or take a more passive or quiet role. You're helping everyone grow in the OUT dimension, but we have to begin where people are, not where we wish they were.

■ Be sensitive to the physical limitations for different OUT activities and consider whether you will be excluding members of your MC in an activity. Perhaps they can provide prayer support onsite or just a friendly smile to those you are serving.

Kids: Be sensitive to the ages of your MC's kids and how they can engage with your OUT activity

MC Gathering Review –

What went well? What would you do differently next time?

_____

_____

_____

_____

_____

_____

_____

_____

_____

_____

_____

_____

_____

_____

_____

Week 1 Summary

☑ UP/IN Gathering
☑ Family Devotion — Developing our IN/OUT rhythms
(What is our Missional Purpose?)

MC Schedule

■ Eat (30 minutes)

Eat (30 min)

_____
_____
_____
_____
_____

■ Thanksgiving (15 minutes)

Thanksgiving (15 min)

_____
_____
_____
_____

■ Singing/Worship (15 minutes)

Worship (15 min)

_____
_____
_____
_____
_____

■ Family Devotion (20 minutes)

Small Group (20 min)

_____

_____

_____

_____

_____

■ Prayer (10 minutes)

Prayer (10 min)

_____

_____

_____

_____

_____

Leader Tips

■ Family Devotion — Developing our IN/OUT rhythms (What is our Missional Purpose?)

- (5 minutes) Intro: Remind the MC that, as Jesus became part of Peter and Andrew's oikos, their **oikos** began to reflect the lifestyle rhythms of Jesus. He helped them to engage with the Father (UP) more effectively, both individually and as a family. He also helped them grow into a family on mission. He trained them how to share what they cultivated together as a family with those who were not yet part of God's family.

- Encourage them that the OUT dimension of life is meant for everyone, regardless of their personality, gift mix, and skill set. All Christians are called to be evangelists and missionaries. This requires that we are open to sharing with others the good things God is giving to us and to love others before we expect them to love God.

- (25 minutes total) Defining your missional purpose: Begin by identifying the Passions and Possessions God has already deposited in your MC to meet the particular Problems in the world around you.

Passions _____

_____

_____

_____

Where do these converge?

Problems _____

_____

_____

Possessions _____

_____

_____

- How to identify your Mission Vision:
  - (10 minutes) Start by asking the group to identify their passions. What excites them? The temptation is to be hyper-spiritual. Maybe they're passionate about fixing cars, or autism, or Crossfit, or football, or racial reconciliation. Write these passions on a small whiteboard or a easel pad so everyone can see what the group is sharing.
  - (10 minutes) Celebrate the diversity of what has been shared, and then ask the MC to get into groups of three to discuss where they think the three areas might converge.
  - (5 minutes) Gather everyone back together and have the groups share what they are seeing. What do they think the MC's Mission Vision might be? Write down these ideas. You might be surprised

to see a clear missional focus begin to emerge, or you may have 2-3 ideas emerge. Remember, Mission Visions can change in different seasons, and discovering your MV in any season can be a matter of experimentation.

- Let the group know the leadership team will spend the week praying over it and share during your next MC what MV you will be running after in that season. You'll have a few weeks to plan the practicalities of your next OUT activity to engage your MV.
  - Below are diagrams of actual Mission Visions from other MCs. This may give you helpful perspective and may be worth sharing with your group to stimulate their thinking.

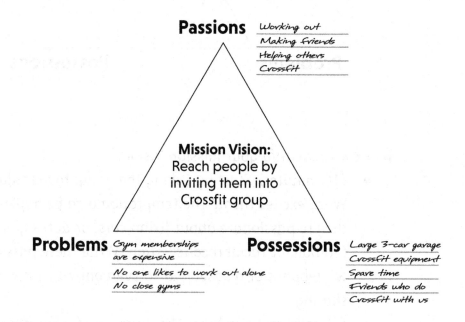

Passions
Working out
Making friends
Helping others
Crossfit

Mission Vision:
Reach people by inviting them into Crossfit group

Problems
Gym memberships are expensive
No one likes to work out alone
No close gyms

Possessions
Large 3-car garage
Crossfit equipment
Spare time
Friends who do Crossfit with us

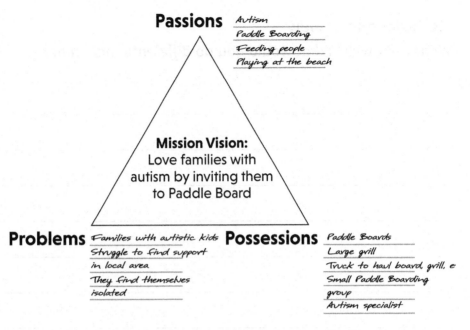

Passions
Autism
Paddle Boarding
Feeding people
Playing at the beach

Mission Vision:
Love families with
autism by inviting them
to Paddle Board

Problems
Families with autistic kids
Struggle to find support
in local area
They find themselves
isolated

Possessions
Paddle Boards
Large grill
Truck to haul board, grill, e
Small Paddle Boarding
group
Autism specialist

- Encourage the group that Jesus did almost all of his evangelism and mission together with his Missional Community—those who were part of his **oikos**, many of whom traveled with him (yes, even women and children). Remind them that you're in this together and that we all get to lean on each other for support and strength.

- Introduce the Mission Vision concept to your MC and engage this exercise as a MC. Feel free to either do the Mission Vision during this gathering or to add another UP/IN week to this interval and focus on this exercise. By this time you have likely been meeting for upward of three months and should be ready to engage well with your Mission Vision. Remember, your MV may change in different seasons. You may revisit your MV every 3-6 months or when you feel your current OUT has grown stagnant.

- Closing: Because of the extra time needed for the MV exercise, you will just want to make sure and close the MC in a timely fashion.

MC Gathering Review —

What went well? What would you do differently next time?

_____

_____

_____

_____

_____

_____

_____

_____

_____

_____

_____

_____

_____

_____

_____

_____

Week 2 Summary

☑ UP/IN Gathering
☑ Small Groups — Praying for POPs

MC Schedule

◼ Eat (30 minutes)

Eat (30 min)

_____

_____

_____

_____

◼ Thanksgiving (15 minutes)

Thanksgiving (15 min)

_____

_____

_____

_____

◼ Singing/Worship (15 minutes)

Worship (15 min)

_____

_____

_____

_____

■ Small Groups (20 minutes)

— Small Group *(20 min)* _____

_____

_____

_____

_____

■ Prayer (10 minutes)

— Prayer *(10 min)* _____

_____

_____

_____

_____

Leader Tips

■ Small Groups — Praying for POPs
  ▪ Remind your MC about the POPs they have identified, and have them take time in their small groups to share about their POPs and pray for them. You can't spend too much time attending to POPs, because this will go far as you develop your OUT dimension as a MC.
  ▪ Once you have given the MC clear instruction, send them into groups of 3-4.

■ Repeat the process of having the core team you are discipling volunteer to lead the small group time. Remember, it's OK to make these groups consistent, or to allow people to gather spontaneously with a different group each time. Find the rhythm that's right for your group.

■ Debrief
  ▪ This is a great time to invite your MC to share any breakthroughs or challenges in their relationships with their POPs. You can share helpful insights and encouragements. Remember, positive testimonies are very powerful to give others fresh hope!

MC Gathering Review –

What went well? What would you do differently next time?

_____

_____

_____

_____

_____

_____

_____

_____

_____

_____

_____

_____

_____

Week 3 Summary

☑ UP/IN Gathering
☑ Small Groups — SG Questions

MC Schedule

■ Eat (30 minutes)

Eat (30 min)

_____

_____

_____

_____

_____

■ Thanksgiving (15 minutes)

Thanksgiving (15 min)

_____

_____

_____

_____

_____

■ Singing/Worship (15 minutes)

Worship (15 min)

_____

_____

_____

_____

_____

■ Small Groups (20 minutes)

Small Group (20 min) _____

_____

_____

_____

_____

■ Prayer (10 minutes)

_____

Prayer (10 min) _____

_____

_____

_____

Leader Tips

■ Small Groups
  - Use the Small Group Questions in the appendix. Make enough copies to share one sheet with each SG, and pass the sheets out as they go into SGs.
  - We instruct members of our MC to get into groups of 3-4 and go through as many of the questions as they have time for.
  - If you have a core team you are discipling and enough to divide the group, then have them raise their hands and let 2-3 others gather with them. They can be your SG leaders. You can encourage these leaders be consistent each time or allow people to gather spontaneously with a different group each time, depending on which seems to work better for your group.

- Debrief
  - Leave 10 minutes at the end of your time together to regroup and share anything from SG that the rest of the family needs to know about. Maybe someone is celebrating a new job or has just found out they have a physical illness or are in need of a new job.
  - We strongly encourage that people share for themselves and not for others. If they say they have permission to share for someone else, I always verify with that person on the spot first.
  - We often take time to quickly pray for some of the things shared in this setting.

MC Gathering Review –

What went well? What would you do differently next time?

_____

_____

_____

_____

_____

_____

_____

_____

_____

_____

_____

_____

_____

_____

Week 4 Summary

- ☑ IN/OUT Gathering
- ☑ OUT Adventure/Mission Vision

MC Schedule

■ You may choose to engage your OUT activity during the usual time of your UP/IN gatherings, or it may make more sense to do it on a different day of the week. During one season our MC met on Wednesday evenings, and our OUT activities were better engaged on the weekends, so that's what we did. On our IN/OUT weeks we have often moved our gathering time to the day/time that was most conducive to our OUT activity.

■ Of course, an OUT gathering your schedule will look different than your UP/IN gatherings. We recommend you gather together first to give clear instruction for the activity and also provide a few minutes on the back end to debrief your experience.
  - Gather for instruction.
  - Engage your Mission Vision (we discuss this fully in Part 1 under IN/OUT Rhythms).
  - Take a few minutes after the activity or at your next MC gathering to debrief the OUT experience with your MC.

Leader Tips

■ We offer lots of ideas in the Appendix that you can try and experiment with. You'll also want to make sure you are throwing a party at least once a month as well. This gives you a minimum of two OUT activities per month. You may do more, but two is a good starting point, especially for those for whom the OUT dimension is more challenging. Remember, predictable patterns like this will create a new culture in your heart and your MC.

■ Make sure to clearly communicate to your MC ahead of time what activity you will be engaging. Does the activity require special accessories like:
  - Walking shoes for a prayer walk
  - Paint brushes, rollers, etc for painting
  - Clean or dirty clothes
  - Games for a party

■ Be appreciative and empathetic with those who are uncomfortable about the OUT activity. Gently encourage them join you, even if they only watch or take a more passive or quiet role. You're helping everyone grow in the OUT dimension, but we have to begin where people are, not where we wish they were.

■ Be sensitive to the physical limitations for different OUT activities and consider whether you will be excluding members of your MC in an activity. Perhaps they can provide prayer support onsite or just a friendly smile to those you are serving.

Kids: Be sensitive to the ages of your MC's kids and how they can engage with your OUT activity

MC Gathering Review —

What went well? What would you do differently next time?

_____

_____

_____

_____

_____

_____

_____

_____

_____

_____

_____

_____

_____

_____

_____

MC ASSESSMENT EXERCISE
UP, IN, OUT Triangle Assessment

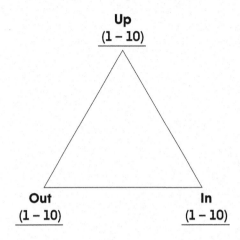

Up
(1 – 10)

Out
(1 – 10)

In
(1 – 10)

(1) Have each member of your team score your MC 1-10 for each of the 3 dimensions.

(2) Have each member share and explain their results. Then process as a team what there is to learn from what is being shared.

(3) Here are some helpful questions to reflect on after you have processed everyone's scores:

- Maintain — What do we need to keep doing that is going well?
- Margin — Where do we need to create space in our MC for new things?
- Maximize — What are we already doing that needs greater intentionality?
- Move into — What do we need to start doing?

Remember, this is a framework in which there is freedom to experiment with and integrate into your MC new activities that may be irregular or regular. Feel free to draw on ideas from the Appendix or others that you have learned. The journey of learning the MC lifestyle is not one of success and failure, but rather of process and learning.

Week 1 Summary

☑ UP/IN Gathering
☑ Family Devotion — Learning to be truly productive

MC Schedule

◼ Eat (30 minutes)

Eat (30 min) ————

_____
_____
_____
_____
_____

◼ Thanksgiving (15 minutes)

Thanksgiving (15 min)

_____
_____
_____
_____
_____

◼ Singing/Worship (15 minutes)

Worship (15 min)

_____
_____
_____
_____
_____

- Family Devotion (20 minutes)

  Small Group (20 min) _____
  _____
  _____
  _____

- Prayer (10 minutes)

  Prayer (10 min) _____
  _____
  _____
  _____
  _____

Leader Tips

- Family Devotion — Learning to be truly productive
  - (15 minutes) — This begins a new Interval which focuses on a new aspect of what it means to be God's family on the earth— **living with a rhythmic lifestyle**. Share with your MC that Jesus was the most productive person to ever walk the earth. We may have more activity in a day than Jesus, but activity doesn't equal productivity. From a kingdom perspective, Jesus was amazingly productive! The question is whether we believe this.

Semi-circle:
Rhythms of Life

Rest   Work

- Too often we see Jesus' life as an anomaly, something beyond our reach. But unless we believe Jesus came to show us a way of being fully human, then we will significantly limit what we can learn from him. Jesus was truly the most productive person! What can we learn from him? After all, Jesus understood how we as humans are made (He had a pretty significant part to play in our design!).

- Read Genesis 2:2, pointing out that God rested on the seventh day of his work. But that happened to be the first day humans had to do anything. So this day, which becomes known as the Sabbath, is a day where we celebrate that God has done everything and that whatever work we will do begins by resting in all that God has already done!

- Use a whiteboard or easel pad to draw the Semi-Circle as a memory aide, and illustrate the two sides REST and WORK.

- Most of us work hard all week and then crash on the weekends, trying to recoup our strength. But this biblical perspective helps us to see that our week begins with rest, rejuvenation, and receiving the strength to step into whatever God has called us to. That's why, in the Hebrew culture, the day starts in the evening. They understand that their day begins with rest (sleep) before they step into all that God has for them in the daytime hours.

- From this we learn that we were created to work from rest, not rest from our work. This is the secret to greater productivity.

- (5 minutes) Q&A

■ Prayer — Make sure to take the last 10 minutes to pray for the sick in your community. This would be a good time to remind them that when we pray for the sick we simply ask the Father for healing and wholeness. Refer to the section in the Part 1 that gives handles for how to introduce simple prayer.

MC Gathering Review –

What went well? What would you do differently next time?

_____

_____

_____

_____

_____

_____

_____

_____

_____

_____

_____

_____

_____

_____

_____

Interval 4 – Finding Fruitfulness

Week 2 Summary

☑ UP/IN Gathering
☑ Small Groups —
   Do I have a healthy personal work/rest rhythm

MC Schedule

■ Eat (30 minutes)

Eat (30 min)

_____

_____

_____

_____

_____

■ Thanksgiving (15 minutes)

Thanksgiving (15 min)

_____

_____

_____

_____

■ Singing/Worship (15 minutes)

Worship (15 min)

_____

_____

_____

_____

■ **Small Groups (20 minutes)**

● ─Small Group (20 min) _____
                         _____

_____

_____

_____

■ **Prayer (10 minutes)**

                         _____
● ─Prayer (10 min)   _____

_____

_____

_____

Leader Tips

■ Small Groups — Do I have a healthy personal work/rest rhythm?
  - (5 minutes) — Remind your MC of some of the key concepts introduced previously about developing healthy rhythms of rest and work. We were created to work from rest, not the other way around.
  - Share briefly about your own journey toward developing these kinds of rhythms. Make sure to share the ups and downs.
  - (15 minutes)— Send the MC into small groups to share about their own daily and weekly rhythms of rest and work. Where are they happy with their rhythms? What would they maybe change? Have the groups pray for one another. Remind them to use their time wisely. A group with three small group participants will have 5 minutes per person for sharing and prayer.

- **Debrief**
  - Gather everyone back together and invite people to share thoughts, questions, and reflections from their small group time. This will give you as leaders a chance to process with them, offer perspective, and encourage.
  - Encourage them to reflect on both their personal rhythms and, for families, how they incorporate daily and weekly family rhythms

MC Gathering Review –

What went well? What would you do differently next time?

_____

_____

_____

_____

_____

_____

_____

_____

_____

_____

_____

_____

_____

_____

Week 3 Summary

☑ UP/IN Gathering
☑ Small Groups — SG Questions

MC Schedule

■ Eat (30 minutes)

_____

_____

_____

_____

■ Thanksgiving (15 minutes)

_____

_____

_____

_____

■ Singing/Worship (15 minutes)

_____

_____

_____

_____

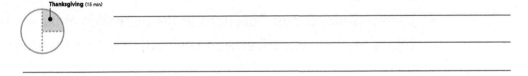

■ **Small Groups (20 minutes)**

Small Group *(20 min)* _____

_____

_____

_____

_____

■ **Prayer (10 minutes)**

Prayer *(10 min)* _____

_____

_____

_____

_____

Leader Tips

■ Small Groups
- Use the Small Group Questions in the appendix. Make enough copies to share one sheet with each SG, and pass the sheets out as they go into SGs.
- We instruct members of our MC to get into groups of 3-4 and go through as many of the questions as they have time for.
- If you have a core team you are discipling and enough to divide the group, then have them raise their hands and let 2-3 others gather with them. They can be your SG leaders. You can encourage these leaders be consistent each time or allow people to gather spontaneously with a different group each time, depending on which seems to work better for your group.

- ■ Debrief
  - ▪ Leave 10 minutes at the end of your time together to regroup and share anything from SG that the rest of the family needs to know about. Maybe someone is celebrating a new job or has just found out they have a physical illness or are in need of a new job.
  - ▪ We strongly encourage that people share for themselves and not for others. If they say they have permission to share for someone else, I always verify with that person on the spot first.
  - ▪ We often take time to quickly pray for some of the things shared in this setting.

MC Gathering Review –

What went well? What would you do differently next time?

_____

_____

_____

_____

_____

_____

_____

_____

_____

_____

_____

_____

_____

_____

_____

_____

Week 4 Summary

☑ IN/OUT Gathering
☑ OUT Adventure/Mission Vision

MC Schedule

■ You may choose to engage your OUT activity during the usual time of your UP/IN gatherings, or it may make more sense to do it on a different day of the week. During one season our MC met on Wednesday evenings, and our OUT activities were better engaged on the weekends, so that's what we did. On our IN/OUT weeks we have often moved our gathering time to the day/time that was most conducive to our OUT activity.

■ Of course, an OUT gathering your schedule will look different than your UP/IN gatherings. We recommend you gather together first to give clear instruction for the activity and also provide a few minutes on the back end to debrief your experience.
  - Gather for instruction.
  - Engage your Mission Vision (we discuss this fully in Part 1 under IN/OUT Rhythms).
  - Take a few minutes after the activity or at your next MC gathering to debrief the OUT experience with your MC.

Leader Tips

- We offer lots of ideas in the Appendix that you can try and experiment with. You'll also want to make sure you are throwing a party at least once a month as well. This gives you a minimum of two OUT activities per month. You may do more, but two is a good starting point, especially for those for whom the OUT dimension is more challenging. Remember, predictable patterns like this will create a new culture in your heart and your MC.

- Make sure to clearly communicate to your MC ahead of time what activity you will be engaging. Does the activity require special accessories like:
  - Walking shoes for a prayer walk
  - Paint brushes, rollers, etc for painting
  - Clean or dirty clothes
  - Games for a party

- Be appreciative and empathetic with those who are uncomfortable about the OUT activity. Gently encourage them join you, even if they only watch or take a more passive or quiet role. You're helping everyone grow in the OUT dimension, but we have to begin where people are, not where we wish they were.

- Be sensitive to the physical limitations for different OUT activities and consider whether you will be excluding members of your MC in an activity. Perhaps they can provide prayer support onsite or just a friendly smile to those you are serving.

  Kids: Be sensitive to the ages of your MC's kids and how they can engage with your OUT activity.

MC Gathering Review —

What went well? What would you do differently next time?

_____

_____

_____

_____

_____

_____

_____

_____

_____

_____

_____

_____

_____

_____

_____

Week 1 Summary

☑ UP/IN Gathering
☑ Family Devotion — The Fruitful Life: Abiding & Fruitfulness

MC Schedule

■ Eat (30 minutes)

_____
_____
_____
_____
_____

■ Thanksgiving (15 minutes)

_____
_____
_____
_____

■ Singing/Worship (15 minutes)

_____
_____
_____
_____

■ Family Devotion (20 minutes)

Small Group (20 min)

_____

_____

_____

_____

■ Prayer (10 minutes)

Prayer (10 min)

_____

_____

_____

_____

Leader Tips

■ Family Devotion — The Fruitful Life: Abiding & Fruitfulness
  - (15 minutes) Take time to read through the chapter from BDC on the Semi-Circle.[17]

Semi-circle:
Rhythms of Life

Abide   **Fruitfulness**

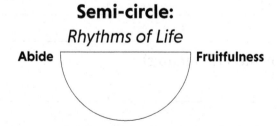

---

[17] Semi-Circle, BDC, Breen

- Read John 15:1-8 and explain to your MC how Jesus is using the relationship between the vine and the branch to help us understand the necessity of the same relationship between us and the Father. As we develop healthy rhythms of abiding (both personal and communal), the natural byproduct is fruit! Fruit trees don't try to produce fruit—they simply do as long as their roots are firmly an-chored in the soil of God's love, grace, mercy, and truth.
- Share about your own journey of learning to abide. What do your personal rhythms look like? What do your household rhythms look like?
- It may be helpful to distinguish between abiding as a spiritual and emotional reali-ty and rest as a physical and mental reality.
- Draw the Semi-Circle again for the group and add to REST and WORK the words ABIDE, FRUIT, PRUNE and GROW.
- (5 minutes) Discussion and Q&A

■ Prayer — Make sure to take the last 10 minutes to pray for the sick in your community. This would be a good time to remind the MC that, when we pray for the sick, we simply ask the Father for healing and wholeness. Refer to the section in the Part 1 that gives handles for how to introduce simple prayer.

MC Gathering Review –

What went well? What would you do differently next time?
What are you learning about leading a MC?

_____

_____

_____

_____

_____

_____

_____

_____

_____

_____

_____

_____

_____

_____

_____

_____

Week 2 Summary

☑ UP/IN Gathering
☑ Small Groups —
    Do I have healthy daily and weekly rhythms of abiding?

MC Schedule

■ Eat (30 minutes)

Eat (30 min)

_____
_____
_____
_____
_____

■ Thanksgiving (15 minutes)

Thanksgiving (15 min)

_____
_____
_____
_____

■ Singing/Worship (15 minutes)

Worship (15 min)

_____
_____
_____
_____

■ Small Groups (20 minutes)

Small Group (20 min) _____

_____

_____

_____

_____

■ Prayer (10 minutes)

Prayer (10 min) _____

_____

_____

_____

Leader Tips

■ Small Groups — Do I have healthy daily and weekly rhythms of abiding
   ▪ (2-3 minutes) Remind your MC of the parable of the vine and branches. Let them know they will be sharing about their personal and household rhythms of abiding. You'll probably want to remind them that this is a journey toward greater fruitfulness, so they'll need to be gracious toward themselves and others.
   ▪ (17 minutes) Send the MC into small groups of 3-4. Have the groups share what their rhythms look like and pray for each other

■ Debrief
   ▪ Gather everyone back together and invite people to share thoughts, questions, and reflections from their SG time. This will give you as leaders a chance to process with them, offer perspective, and encourage.

- Encourage them to reflect on both their personal rhythms and, for families, how they incorporate daily and weekly family rhythms.

MC Gathering Review –
What went well? What would you do differently next time?
What are you learning about leading a MC?

_____

_____

_____

_____

_____

_____

_____

_____

_____

_____

_____

_____

_____

Week 3 Summary

☑ UP/IN Gathering
☑ Small Groups — SG Questions or Other

MC Schedule

■ Eat (30 minutes)

Eat (30 min)

_____
_____

■ Thanksgiving (15 minutes)

Thanksgiving (15 min)

_____
_____

■ Singing/Worship (15 minutes)

Worship (15 min)

_____
_____

■ Small Groups (20 minutes)

⌒ ●—**Small Group** *(20 min)* _____

_____

_____

_____

_____

■ Prayer (10 minutes)

⌒ ●—**Prayer** *(10 min)* _____

_____

_____

_____

_____

Leader Tips

■ Small Groups
- Use the Small Group Questions in the appendix. Make enough copies to share one sheet with each SG, and pass the sheets out as they go into SGs.
- We instruct members of our MC to get into groups of 3-4 and go through as many of the questions as they have time for.
- If you have a core team you are discipling and enough to divide the group, then have them raise their hands and let 2-3 others gather with them. They can be your SG leaders. You can encourage these leaders be consistent each time or allow people to gather spontaneously with a different group each time, depending on which seems to work better for your group.

- Debrief
    - Leave 10 minutes at the end of your time together to regroup and share anything from SG that the rest of the family needs to know about. Maybe someone is celebrating a new job or has just found out they have a physical illness or are in need of a new job.
    - We strongly encourage that people share for themselves and not for others. If they say they have permission to share for someone else, I always verify with that person on the spot first.
    - We often take time to quickly pray for some of the things shared in this setting.

MC Gathering Review –

What went well? What would you do differently next time?

_____

_____

_____

_____

_____

_____

_____

_____

_____

_____

_____

_____

_____

_____

Week 4 Summary

☑ IN/OUT Gathering
☑ OUT Adventure/Mission Vision

MC Schedule

■ You may choose to engage your OUT activity during the usual time of your UP/IN gatherings, or it may make more sense to do it on a different day of the week. During one season our MC met on Wednesday evenings, and our OUT activities were better engaged on the weekends, so that's what we did. On our IN/OUT weeks we have often moved our gathering time to the day/time that was most conducive to our OUT activity.

■ Of course, an OUT gathering your schedule will look different than your UP/IN gatherings. We recommend you gather together first to give clear instruction for the activity and also provide a few minutes on the back end to debrief your experience.
- Gather for instruction.
- Engage your Mission Vision (we discuss this fully in Part 1 under IN/OUT Rhythms).
- Take a few minutes after the activity or at your next MC gathering to debrief the OUT experience with your MC.

Leader Tips

- We offer lots of ideas in the Appendix that you can try and experiment with. You'll also want to make sure you are throwing a party at least once a month as well. This gives you a minimum of two OUT activities per month. You may do more, but two is a good starting point, especially for those for whom the OUT dimension is more challenging. Remember, predictable patterns like this will create a new culture in your heart and your MC.

- Make sure to clearly communicate to your MC ahead of time what activity you will be engaging. Does the activity require special accessories like:
  - Walking shoes for a prayer walk
  - Paint brushes, rollers, etc for painting
  - Clean or dirty clothes
  - Games for a party

- Be appreciative and empathetic with those who are uncomfortable about the OUT activity. Gently encourage them join you, even if they only watch or take a more passive or quiet role. You're helping everyone grow in the OUT dimension, but we have to begin where people are, not where we wish they were.

- Be sensitive to the physical limitations for different OUT activities and consider whether you will be excluding members of your MC in an activity. Perhaps they can provide prayer support onsite or just a friendly smile to those you are serving.

  Kids: Be sensitive to the ages of your MC's kids and how they can engage with your OUT activity.

MC Gathering Review —

What went well? What would you do differently next time?

_____

_____

_____

_____

_____

_____

_____

_____

_____

_____

_____

_____

_____

_____

_____

_____

Week 1 Summary

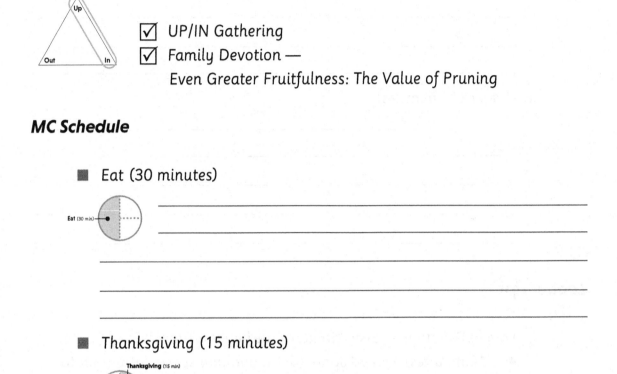

☑ UP/IN Gathering
☑ Family Devotion —
  Even Greater Fruitfulness: The Value of Pruning

MC Schedule

■ Eat (30 minutes)

_____
_____
_____
_____
_____

■ Thanksgiving (15 minutes)

_____
_____
_____
_____

■ Singing/Worship (15 minutes)

_____
_____
_____
_____

■ Family Devotion (20 minutes)

Small Group (20 min)

_____

_____

_____

_____

_____

■ Prayer (10 minutes)

Prayer (10 min)

_____

_____

_____

_____

_____

Leader Tips

■ Family Devotion — Even Greater Fruitfulness: The Value of Pruning
   - (10 minutes) Reread John 15:1-8 and pay special attention to verse 2. Help your MC understand how the vinedresser prunes branches each season. Some are pruned so they can be more fruitful, and others are pruned because they are sucking life from the vine and cheating the other branches of vitality. It is important to identify which areas of our lives God is causing to grow, and which are being pruned.
   - (5 minutes) Invite everyone to take a few minutes to reflect on which areas of their life God seems to be growing and which he may be pruning.
   - (5 minutes) Discussion and Q&A

■ Prayer — Make sure to take the last 10 minutes to pray for the sick in your community. This would be a good time to remind the MC that, when we pray for the sick, we simply ask the Father for healing and wholeness.

MC Gathering Review –

What went well? What would you do differently next time?

_____

_____

_____

_____

_____

_____

_____

_____

_____

_____

_____

_____

_____

_____

Interval 6 — Finding Fruitfulness 6.2

Week 2 Summary

☑ UP/IN Gathering
☑ Small Groups — Embracing the value of pruning

MC Schedule

■ Eat (30 minutes)

Eat (30 min)

_____

_____

_____

_____

_____

■ Thanksgiving (15 minutes)

Thanksgiving (15 min)

_____

_____

_____

_____

_____

■ Singing/Worship (15 minutes)

Worship (15 min)

_____

_____

_____

_____

_____

■ Small Groups (20 minutes)

Small Group (20 min) _____

_____

_____

_____

_____

■ Prayer (10 minutes)

Prayer (10 min) _____

_____

_____

_____

_____

Leader Tips

■ Small Groups — Embracing the value of pruning
- (3-5 minutes) Remind the group the Semi-Circle and the necessity of allowing God to prune areas of our lives for greater fruitfulness. Share some of your own experiences of having areas of your life pruned.

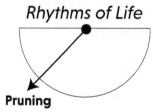

Semi-circle:

Rhythms of Life

Pruning

- (15 minutes) Let the MC know you are sending them into small groups to share areas they believe are being pruned or need to be pruned. Have the groups pray for each other.

■ Debrief
  ▪ Gather everyone back together and invite people to share thoughts, questions and reflections from their small group time. This will give you as leaders a chance to process with them, offer perspective, and encourage.

MC Gathering Review –

What went well? What would you do differently next time?
What are you learning about leading a MC?

_____

_____

_____

_____

_____

_____

_____

_____

_____

_____

_____

_____

_____

_____

Week 3 Summary

☑ UP/IN Gathering
☑ Small Groups — SG Questions or Other

MC Schedule

■ Eat (30 minutes)

Eat (30 min)

_____

_____

_____

_____

■ Thanksgiving (15 minutes)

Thanksgiving (15 min)

_____

_____

_____

_____

■ Singing/Worship (15 minutes)

Worship (15 min)

_____

_____

_____

_____

■ Small Groups (20 minutes)

Small Group (20 min) _____

_____

_____

_____

■ Prayer (10 minutes)

Prayer (10 min) _____

_____

_____

_____

Leader Tips

■ Small Groups
  ■ Use the Small Group Questions in the appendix. Make enough copies to share one sheet with each SG, and pass the sheets out as they go into SGs.
  ■ We instruct members of our MC to get into groups of 3-4 and go through as many of the questions as they have time for.
  ■ If you have a core team you are discipling and enough to divide the group, then have them raise their hands and let 2-3 others gather with them. They can be your SG leaders. You can encourage these leaders be consistent each time or allow people to gather spontaneously with a different group each time, depending on which seems to work better for your group.

- Debrief
  - Leave 10 minutes at the end of your time together to regroup and share anything from SG that the rest of the family needs to know about. Maybe someone is celebrating a new job or has just found out they have a physical illness or are in need of a new job.
  - We strongly encourage that people share for themselves and not for others. If they say they have permission to share for someone else, I always verify with that person on the spot first.
  - We often take time to quickly pray for some of the things shared in this setting.

MC Gathering Review —

What went well? What would you do differently next time?

_____

_____

_____

_____

_____

_____

_____

_____

_____

_____

_____

_____

_____

_____

_____

Week 4 Summary

☑ IN/OUT Gathering
☑ OUT Adventure/Mission Vision

MC Schedule

■ You may choose to engage your OUT activity during the usual time of your UP/IN gatherings, or it may make more sense to do it on a different day of the week. During one season our MC met on Wednesday evenings, and our OUT activities were better engaged on the weekends, so that's what we did. On our IN/OUT weeks we have often moved our gathering time to the day/time that was most conducive to our OUT activity.

■ Of course, an OUT gathering your schedule will look different than your UP/IN gatherings. We recommend you gather together first to give clear instruction for the activity and also provide a few minutes on the back end to debrief your experience.

  • Gather for instruction.
  • Engage your Mission Vision (we discuss this fully in Part 1 under IN/OUT Rhythms).
  • Take a few minutes after the activity or at your next MC gathering to debrief the OUT experience with your MC.

Leader Tips

■ We offer lots of ideas in the Appendix that you can try and experiment with. You'll also want to make sure you are throwing a party at least once a month as well. This gives you a minimum of two OUT activities per month. You may do more, but two is a good starting point, especially for those for whom the OUT dimension is more challenging. Remember, predictable patterns like this will create a new culture in your heart and your MC.

■ Make sure to clearly communicate to your MC ahead of time what activity you will be engaging. Does the activity require special accessories like:
  - Walking shoes for a prayer walk
  - Paint brushes, rollers, etc for painting
  - Clean or dirty clothes
  - Games for a party

■ Be appreciative and empathetic with those who are uncomfortable about the OUT activi-ty. Gently encourage them join you, even if they only watch or take a more passive or quiet role. You're helping everyone grow in the OUT dimension, but we have to begin where people are, not where we wish they were.

■ Be sensitive to the physical limitations for different OUT activities and consider whether you will be excluding members of your MC in an activity. Perhaps they can provide prayer support onsite or just a friendly smile to those you are serving.

Kids: Be sensitive to the ages of your MC's kids and how they can engage with your OUT activity.

MC Gathering Review —

What went well? What would you do differently next time?

_____

_____

_____

_____

_____

_____

_____

_____

_____

_____

_____

_____

_____

_____

_____

MC ASSESSMENT EXERCISE
UP, IN, OUT Triangle Assessment

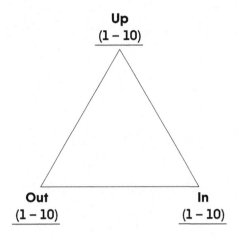

Up
(1 – 10)

Out
(1 – 10)

In
(1 – 10)

(1) Have each member of your team score your MC 1-10 for each of the 3 dimensions.

(2) Have each member share and explain their results. Then process as a team what there is to learn from what is being shared.

(3) Here are some helpful questions to reflect on after you have processed everyone's scores:

- Maintain — What do we need to keep doing that is going well?
- Margin — Where do we need to create space in our MC for new things?
- Maximize — What are we already doing that needs greater intentionality?
- Move into — What do we need to start doing?

Remember, this is a framework in which there is freedom to experiment with and integrate into your MC new activities that may be irregular or regular. Feel free to draw on ideas from the Appendix or others that you have learned. The journey of learning the MC lifestyle is not one of success and failure, but rather of process and learning.

Week 1 Summary

☑ UP/IN Gathering
☑ Family Devotion —
    The Empowered Life: Invitation & Challenge

MC Schedule

■ Eat (30 minutes)

_____
_____
_____
_____
_____

■ Thanksgiving (15 minutes)

_____
_____
_____
_____

■ Singing/Worship (15 minutes)

_____
_____
_____
_____

■ Family Devotion (20 minutes)

●—**Small Group** (20 min) _____

_____

_____

_____

_____

■ Prayer (10 minutes)

●—**Prayer** (10 min) _____

_____

_____

_____

_____

Leader Tips

■ Family Devotion — The Empowered Life: Invitation & Challenge
  - You can review the concepts of Invitation & Challenge in BDC.[18]
  - (5 minutes) Introducing Invitation & Challenge:
    - Take a few minutes to share how God helps us grow by inviting us to share in more of his family blessings and challenging to take greater responsibility within the "family business." Talk about how God calibrates these thigns together.
    - Read from a scripture of your choice that illustrates both invitation and challenge. Some classic stories we use are Matthew 16:13-23, Mark 10:17-29, and Luke 15:11-32.

---

[18] Invitation & Challenge, BDC, Breen

- (10 minutes) Draw the Invitation & Challenge Matrix for the group and identify each of the four quadrants. Show how this is a helpful way of illustrating how God leads us, but also what happens when we only emphasize invitation or challenge.

- Ask the MC to identify which quadrant they believe best represents their current relationship with God. Ask them to identify which quadrant represents how others might experience your MC.
- (5 minutes) Discuss and Q&A

MC Gathering Review —

What went well? What would you do differently next time?
What are you learning about leading a MC?

_____

_____

_____

_____

_____

_____

_____

_____

_____

_____

_____

_____

_____

_____

Week 2 Summary

☑ UP/IN Gathering
☑ Small Groups — Is God inviting me or challenging me?

MC Schedule

■ Eat (30 minutes)

Eat (30 min)

_____
_____
_____
_____
_____

■ Thanksgiving (15 minutes)

Thanksgiving (15 min)

_____
_____
_____
_____
_____

■ Singing/Worship (15 minutes)

Worship (15 min)

_____
_____
_____
_____
_____

■ Small Groups (20 minutes)

■ Small Group (20 min) _____

_____

_____

_____

_____

■ Prayer (10 minutes)

■ Prayer (10 min) _____

_____

_____

_____

Leader Tips

■ Small Groups — Is God inviting me or challenging me?
  ■ (3-5 minutes) — Remind the group of the importance of allowing God to both invite and challenge us if we are going to grow. I find it helpful to ask people to imagine a trainer at the gym who only calibrates invitation or challenge. Would such a trainer be very effective to help someone grow in their fitness?
  ■ (15 minutes) — Send the MC in to small groups to share where they believe God is inviting them or challenging them. Take time to encourage and pray for each other.

■ Debrief
  ■ Gather everyone back together and invite people to share thoughts, questions, and reflections from their small group time. This will give you as leaders a chance to process with them, offer perspective, and encourage.

MC Gathering Review –

What went well? What would you do differently next time?
What are you learning about leading a MC?

_____

_____

_____

_____

_____

_____

_____

_____

_____

_____

_____

_____

_____

Week 3 Summary

☑ UP/IN Gathering
☑ Small Groups — SG Questions or Other

MC Schedule

■ Eat (30 minutes)

_____
_____
_____
_____
_____

■ Thanksgiving (15 minutes)

_____
_____
_____
_____
_____

■ Singing/Worship (15 minutes)

_____
_____
_____
_____
_____

■ Small Groups (20 minutes)

Small Group (20 min) _____

_____

_____

_____

_____

■ Prayer (10 minutes)

Prayer (10 min) _____

_____

_____

_____

_____

Leader Tips

■ Small Groups
- Use the Small Group Questions in the appendix. Make enough copies to share one sheet with each SG, and pass the sheets out as they go into SGs.
- We instruct members of our MC to get into groups of 3-4 and go through as many of the questions as they have time for.
- If you have a core team you are discipling and enough to divide the group, then have them raise their hands and let 2-3 others gather with them. They can be your SG leaders. You can encourage these leaders be consistent each time or allow people to gather spontaneously with a different group each time, depending on which seems to work better for your group.

■ Debrief
  ▪ Leave 10 minutes at the end of your time together to regroup and share anything from SG that the rest of the family needs to know about. Maybe someone is celebrating a new job or has just found out they have a physical illness or are in need of a new job.
  ▪ We strongly encourage that people share for themselves and not for others. If they say they have permission to share for someone else, I always verify with that person on the spot first.
  ▪ We often take time to quickly pray for some of the things shared in this setting.

MC Gathering Review —

What went well? What would you do differently next time?

_____

_____

_____

_____

_____

_____

_____

_____

_____

_____

_____

_____

_____

_____

_____

Week 4 Summary

☑ IN/OUT Gathering
☑ OUT Adventure/Mission Vision

MC Schedule

■ You may choose to engage your OUT activity during the usual time of your UP/IN gath-erings, or it may make more sense to do it on a different day of the week. During one season our MC met on Wednesday evenings, and our OUT activities were better engaged on the weekends, so that's what we did. On our IN/OUT weeks we have often moved our gathering time to the day/time that was most conducive to our OUT activity.

■ Of course, an OUT gathering your schedule will look different than your UP/IN gatherings. We recommend you gather together first to give clear instruction for the activity and also provide a few minutes on the back end to debrief your experience.

  ▪ Gather for instruction.
  ▪ Engage your Mission Vision (we discuss this fully in Part 1 under IN/OUT Rhythms).
  ▪ Take a few minutes after the activity or at your next MC gathering to debrief the OUT experience with your MC.

Leader Tips

- We offer lots of ideas in the Appendix that you can try and experiment with. You'll also want to make sure you are throwing a party at least once a month as well. This gives you a minimum of two OUT activities per month. You may do more, but two is a good starting point, especially for those for whom the OUT dimension is more challenging. Remember, predictable patterns like this will create a new culture in your heart and your MC.

- Make sure to clearly communicate to your MC ahead of time what activity you will be engaging. Does the activity require special accessories like:
  - Walking shoes for a prayer walk
  - Paint brushes, rollers, etc for painting
  - Clean or dirty clothes
  - Games for a party

- Be appreciative and empathetic with those who are uncomfortable about the OUT activity. Gently encourage them join you, even if they only watch or take a more passive or quiet role. You're helping everyone grow in the OUT dimension, but we have to begin where people are, not where we wish they were.

- Be sensitive to the physical limitations for different OUT activities and consider whether you will be excluding members of your MC in an activity. Perhaps they can provide prayer support onsite or just a friendly smile to those you are serving.

    Kids: Be sensitive to the ages of your MC's kids and how they can engage with your OUT activity.

MC Gathering Review —

What went well? What would you do differently next time?

_____

_____

_____

_____

_____

_____

_____

_____

_____

_____

_____

_____

_____

_____

_____

Week 1 Summary

☑ UP/IN Gathering
☑ Family Devotion —
 Empowering Others: Leading with Invitation & Challenge

MC Schedule

■ Eat (30 minutes)

_____
_____

_____
_____
_____

■ Thanksgiving (15 minutes)

_____
_____

_____
_____
_____

■ Singing/Worship (15 minutes)

_____
_____

_____
_____

■ Family Devotion (20 minutes)

Small Group (20 min) _____

_____

_____

_____

_____

■ Prayer (10 minutes)

Prayer (10 min) _____

_____

_____

_____

_____

Leader Tips

■ Family Devotion — Empowering Others: Leading with Invitation & Challenge

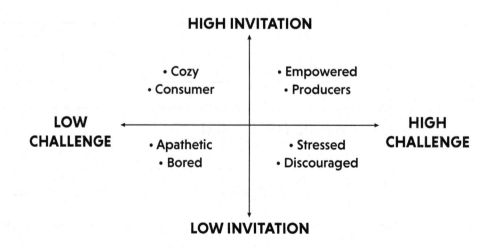

- (15 minutes) Take time to review the Invitation & Challenge Matrix and the four quadrants. Share with the MC that all of us have a preference for invitation or challenge and that we influence others by how we calibrate invitation and challenge with them. Are we empowering others? Remind them that leaders define their culture, and that includes parents their own households.
- Ask the MC these questions: Which do you think you are better at calibrating? How do you know? How is your leadership reflected in the contexts in which you have influence (such as home life, at work, at school, etc)? Process their responses in the group.
- (5 minutes) Take some time to share how they can grow in their area of weakness. Ideas:
  - Find someone that is better than you at invitation or challenge and imitate how that person expresses it.
  - As you read the Scripture, pay attention to how God invites and challenges his people. How does Jesus calibrate both with his disciples?

- Prayer — You may want to pray for the sick in your MC or spend time praying for those who want to grow in invitation or challenge.

MC Gathering Review –

What went well? What would you do differently next time?
What are you learning about leading a MC?

_____

_____

_____

_____

_____

_____

_____

_____

_____

_____

_____

_____

_____

Week 2 Summary

- ☑ UP/IN Gathering
- ☑ Small Groups —
  Empowering Others: Leading with Invitation & Challenge

MC Schedule

■ Eat (30 minutes)

Eat (30 min)

_____

_____

_____

_____

_____

■ Thanksgiving (15 minutes)

Thanksgiving (15 min)

_____

_____

_____

_____

■ Singing/Worship (15 minutes)

Worship (15 min)

_____

_____

_____

_____

■ Small Groups (20 minutes)

Small Group (20 min) _____

_____

_____

_____

_____

■ Prayer (10 minutes)

Prayer (10 min) _____

_____

_____

_____

_____

Leader Tips

■ Small Groups — Is God inviting me or challenging me?
- (3-5 minutes) Remind the group how we create the culture around us by how we calibrate invitation and challenge. Share from your own journey of how you are learning to calibrate both more effectively. It helps to share from both your failures and successes.
- (15 minutes) Send the MC to small groups to share how they see their leadership affecting the contexts they lead in, and to pray for each other.

■ Debrief
- Gather everyone back together and invite people to share thoughts, questions and reflections from their small group time. This will give you as leaders a chance to process with them, offer perspective, and encourage.

MC Gathering Review —

What went well? What would you do differently next time?
What are you learning about leading a MC?

_____

_____

_____

_____

_____

_____

_____

_____

_____

_____

_____

_____

_____

_____

_____

Week 3 Summary

☑ UP/IN Gathering
☑ Small Groups — SG Questions or Other

MC Schedule

■ Eat (30 minutes)

_____

_____

_____

_____

_____

■ Thanksgiving (15 minutes)

_____

_____

_____

_____

_____

■ Singing/Worship (15 minutes)

_____

_____

_____

_____

_____

■ Small Groups (20 minutes)

⟞ Small Group (20 min) _____

_____

_____

_____

_____

■ Prayer (10 minutes)

⟞ Prayer (10 min) _____

_____

_____

_____

_____

Leader Tips

■ Small Groups
- Use the Small Group Questions in the appendix. Make enough copies to share one sheet with each SG, and pass the sheets out as they go into SGs.
- We instruct members of our MC to get into groups of 3-4 and go through as many of the questions as they have time for.
- If you have a core team you are discipling and enough to divide the group, then have them raise their hands and let 2-3 others gather with them. They can be your SG leaders. You can encourage these leaders be consistent each time or allow people to gather spontaneously with a different group each time, depending on which seems to work better for your group.

■ Debrief
  ▪ Leave 10 minutes at the end of your time together to regroup and share anything from SG that the rest of the family needs to know about. Maybe someone is celebrating a new job or has just found out they have a physical illness or are in need of a new job.
  ▪ We strongly encourage that people share for themselves and not for others. If they say they have permission to share for someone else, I always verify with that person on the spot first.
  ▪ We often take time to quickly pray for some of the things shared in this setting

MC Gathering Review –

What went well? What would you do differently next time?

_____

_____

_____

_____

_____

_____

_____

_____

_____

_____

_____

_____

_____

Week 4 Summary

☑ IN/OUT Gathering
☑ OUT Adventure/Mission Vision

MC Schedule

■ You may choose to engage your OUT activity during the usual time of your UP/IN gatherings, or it may make more sense to do it on a different day of the week. During one season our MC met on Wednesday evenings, and our OUT activities were better engaged on the weekends, so that's what we did. On our IN/OUT weeks we have often moved our gathering time to the day/time that was most conducive to our OUT activity.

■ Of course, an OUT gathering your schedule will look different than your UP/IN gatherings. We recommend you gather together first to give clear instruction for the activity and also provide a few minutes on the back end to debrief your experience.
  ■ Gather for instruction.
  ■ Engage your Mission Vision (we discuss this fully in Part 1 under IN/OUT Rhythms).
  ■ Take a few minutes after the activity or at your next MC gathering to debrief the OUT experience with your MC.

Leader Tips

■ We offer lots of ideas in the Appendix that you can try and experiment with. You'll also want to make sure you are throwing a party at least once a month as well. This gives you a minimum of two OUT activities per month. You may do more, but two is a good starting point, especially for those for whom the OUT dimension is more challenging. Remember, predictable patterns like this will create a new culture in your heart and your MC.

■ Make sure to clearly communicate to your MC ahead of time what activity you will be engaging. Does the activity require special accessories like:
  - Walking shoes for a prayer walk
  - Paint brushes, rollers, etc for painting
  - Clean or dirty clothes
  - Games for a party

■ Be appreciative and empathetic with those who are uncomfortable about the OUT activity. Gently encourage them join you, even if they only watch or take a more passive or quiet role. You're helping everyone grow in the OUT dimension, but we have to begin where people are, not where we wish they were.

■ Be sensitive to the physical limitations for different OUT activities and consider whether you will be excluding members of your MC in an activity. Perhaps they can provide prayer support onsite or just a friendly smile to those you are serving.

  Kids: Be sensitive to the ages of your MC's kids and how they can engage with your OUT activity.

MC Gathering Review –

What went well? What would you do differently next time?

_____

_____

_____

_____

_____

_____

_____

_____

_____

_____

_____

_____

_____

_____

_____

MC Gathering Review –

What went well? What would you do differently next time?

_____

_____

_____

_____

_____

_____

_____

_____

_____

_____

_____

_____

_____

_____

Interval 9 — The Empowered Life

Week 1 Summary

☑ UP/IN Gathering
☑ Family Devotion —
  Being an Empowering Community: Family on Mission

MC Schedule

■ Eat (30 minutes)

_____
_____
_____
_____
_____

■ Thanksgiving (15 minutes)

_____
_____
_____
_____

■ Singing/Worship (15 minutes)

_____
_____
_____
_____

■ Family Devotion (20 minutes)

Small Group (20 min)

_____

_____

_____

_____

_____

■ Prayer (10 minutes)

Prayer (10 min)

_____

_____

_____

_____

Leader Tips

■ Family Devotion — Being an Empowering Community:
Family on Mission
- (20 minutes) Remind your MC that the heart of God is to empower us by graciously calibrating increasing invitation and challenge as we learn more and more about what it means to be part of his Family on Mission. As an MC we get to represent God's family on mission! As they are exposed to our MC, others should get a better picture of who God is and how he operates..
- Ask the following questions of the group:
  - What is inviting about our MC? Do we offer support, care, provision, nurture, encouragement, etc?
  - What is challenging about our MC? Are more people taking greater responsibility? Are people moving beyond their comfort zone?

- Are we better as an MC at invitation or challenge? How is this affecting our ability to grow as a Family on Mission?
- Are we developing in all three dimensions of the life of Jesus: UP, IN, OUT?
- Are we learning to engage better rhythms of life both personally and as households? Are we more fruitful today than we were when we started in this journey?

■ Allow these questions to fuel a group-wide discussion.

■ This discussion should give the leaders some handles for how to invest into the MC.

MC Gathering Review —

What went well? What would you do differently next time?
What are you learning about leading a MC?

_____

_____

_____

_____

_____

_____

_____

_____

_____

_____

_____

_____

_____

_____

Week 2 Summary

☑ UP/IN Gathering
☑ Small Groups — Where am I being empowered?

MC Schedule

■ Eat (30 minutes)

_____
_____
_____
_____
_____

■ Thanksgiving (15 minutes)

_____
_____
_____
_____
_____

■ Singing/Worship (15 minutes)

_____
_____
_____
_____
_____

Small Groups (20 minutes)

Small Group (20 min)

_____

_____

_____

_____

_____

Prayer (10 minutes)

Prayer (10 min)

_____

_____

_____

_____

_____

Leader Tips

- Small Groups — Where am I being empowered?
  - (20 minutes) Send the MC into small groups (you know how to do this now!) to share where they believe they are growing as a result of being part of the MC. These areas of growth can be small or big. This should be a time of encouragement.

- Debrief
  - Gather everyone back together and invite people to share where they have grown. Take time to affirm them, and also don't be afraid to point out where you as the leaders have seen different people grow.

MC Gathering Review —

What went well? What would you do differently next time?
What are you learning about leading a MC?

_____

_____

_____

_____

_____

_____

_____

_____

_____

_____

_____

_____

_____

_____

_____

_____

Week 3 Summary

☑ UP/IN Gathering
☑ Small Groups — SG Questions or Other

MC Schedule

■ Eat (30 minutes)

Eat (30 min)

_____
_____
_____
_____
_____

■ Thanksgiving (15 minutes)

Thanksgiving (15 min)

_____
_____
_____
_____
_____

■ Singing/Worship (15 minutes)

Worship (15 min)

_____
_____
_____
_____
_____

■ Small Groups (20 minutes)

Small Group (20 min) _____

_____

_____

_____

_____

■ Prayer (10 minutes)

Prayer (10 min) _____

_____

_____

_____

_____

Leader Tips

■ Small Groups
- Use the Small Group Questions in the appendix. Make enough copies to share one sheet with each SG, and pass the sheets out as they go into SGs.
- We instruct members of our MC to get into groups of 3-4 and go through as many of the questions as they have time for.
- If you have a core team you are discipling and enough to divide the group, then have them raise their hands and let 2-3 others gather with them. They can be your SG leaders. You can encourage these leaders be consistent each time or allow people to gather spontaneously with a different group each time, depending on which seems to work better for your group.

■ Debrief
  ▪ Leave 10 minutes at the end of your time together to regroup and share anything from SG that the rest of the family needs to know about. Maybe someone is celebrating a new job or has just found out they have a physical illness or are in need of a new job.
  ▪ We strongly encourage that people share for themselves and not for others. If they say they have permission to share for someone else, I always verify with that person on the spot first.
  ▪ We often take time to quickly pray for some of the things shared in this setting.

MC Gathering Review –

What went well? What would you do differently next time?

_____

_____

_____

_____

_____

_____

_____

_____

_____

_____

_____

_____

_____

_____

Week 4 Summary

☑ IN/OUT Gathering
☑ OUT Adventure/Mission Vision

MC Schedule

◾ You may choose to engage your OUT activity during the usual time of your UP/IN gatherings, or it may make more sense to do it on a different day of the week. During one season our MC met on Wednesday evenings, and our OUT activities were better engaged on the weekends, so that's what we did. On our IN/OUT weeks we have often moved our gathering time to the day/time that was most conducive to our OUT activity.

◾ Of course, an OUT gathering your schedule will look different than your UP/IN gatherings. We recommend you gather together first to give clear instruction for the activity and also provide a few minutes on the back end to debrief your experience.

- Gather for instruction.
- Engage your Mission Vision (we discuss this fully in Part 1 under IN/OUT Rhythms).
- Take a few minutes after the activity or at your next MC gathering to debrief the OUT experience with your MC.

Leader Tips

■ We offer lots of ideas in the Appendix that you can try and experiment with. You'll also want to make sure you are throwing a party at least once a month as well. This gives you a minimum of two OUT activities per month. You may do more, but two is a good starting point, especially for those for whom the OUT dimension is more challenging. Remember, predictable patterns like this will create a new culture in your heart and your MC.

■ Make sure to clearly communicate to your MC ahead of time what activity you will be engaging. Does the activity require special accessories like:
  - Walking shoes for a prayer walk
  - Paint brushes, rollers, etc for painting
  - Clean or dirty clothes
  - Games for a party

■ Be appreciative and empathetic with those who are uncomfortable about the OUT activity. Gently encourage them join you, even if they only watch or take a more passive or quiet role. You're helping everyone grow in the OUT dimension, but we have to begin where people are, not where we wish they were.

■ Be sensitive to the physical limitations for different OUT activities and consider whether you will be excluding members of your MC in an activity. Perhaps they can provide prayer support onsite or just a friendly smile to those you are serving.

Kids: Be sensitive to the ages of your MC's kids and how they can engage with your OUT activity.

MC Gathering Review —

What went well? What would you do differently next time?

_____

_____

_____

_____

_____

_____

_____

_____

_____

_____

_____

_____

_____

_____

_____

MC ASSESSMENT EXERCISE
UP, IN, OUT Triangle Assessment

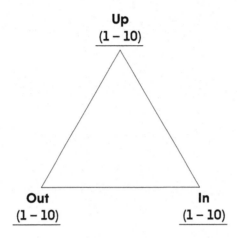

(1) Have each member of your team score your MC 1-10 for each of the 3 dimensions.

(2) Have each member share and explain their results. Then process as a team what there is to learn from what is being shared.

(3) Here are some helpful questions to reflect on after you have processed everyone's scores:

- Maintain — What do we need to keep doing that is going well?
- Margin — Where do we need to create space in our MC for new things?
- Maximize — What are we already doing that needs greater intentionality?
- Move into — What do we need to start doing?

Remember, this is a framework in which there is freedom to experiment with and integrate into your MC new activities that may be irregular or regular. Feel free to draw on ideas from the Appendix or others that you have learned. The journey of learning the MC lifestyle is not one of success and failure, but rather of process and learning.

Week 1 Summary

☑ UP/IN Gathering
☑ Family Devotion — Praying like Jesus

MC Schedule

■ Eat (30 minutes)

_____
_____
_____
_____
_____

■ Thanksgiving (15 minutes)

_____
_____
_____
_____
_____

■ Singing/Worship (15 minutes)

_____
_____
_____
_____
_____

■ Family Devotion (20 minutes)

◗ —Small Group (20 min) _____

_____

_____

_____

_____

■ Prayer (10 minutes)

◗ —Prayer (10 min) _____

_____

_____

_____

Leader Tips

■ Family Devotion — Praying like Jesus
  - (15 minutes) We all have different experiences with prayer. Some of us enjoy praying, while others don't. Some are comfortable praying out loud, and others are not. Some of received training in prayer, while others are still praying the same way they did when they were kids. Either way, the heart of Jesus is that we grow like he did in our ability to engage the Father—this is prayer.
  - Jesus said over and over that the power of his life flowed from this posture—he only ever said what he heard the Father saying and did what he saw the Father doing. This means Jesus was able to engage the Father to see and hear him and then respond.
  - Guess what? This is exactly how we are meant to engage the Father. But like Jesus we have to grow into it. It's easy to forget the 30 years that Jesus was growing in these areas before the Gospel stories begin!

- We're going to learn a simple way of learning to see and hear the Father. Think of this as practice, not performance.
- Read Matthew 6:9-13 then draw the Hexagon.[19] Introduce the 6 words that remind us who God is and how we engage him.

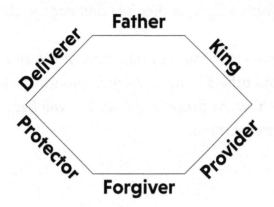

Explain a bit about each one:

Father: "Our Father who is in heaven, hallowed be your name"

King: "Your kingdom come, your will be done on earth as it is in heaven"

Provider: "Give us today our daily bread"

Forgiver: "Forgive us our debts/trespasses as we forgive our debtors/those who trespass against us"

Protector: "Lead us not into temptation"

Deliverer: "Deliver us from the evil one"

- (5 minutes) Invite the group to reflect on which of these aspects of God they are most comfortable with and which they are least comfortable with. Discuss. This will give you as leaders a better understanding of where your group is.

---

[19] Hexagon, BDC, Breen

- Each of these phrases helps us to understand who God is and what we can expect of him as our Father and King. Everyone in your MC will have different experiences with this prayer and how they engage God, so this is your opportunity to begin to shape in a fresh way how they see and engage God

- Prayer — Make sure to take time at the end of the MC to pray for the sick and others in need. As you unpack the Hexagon, you will begin to see how the prayers of your MC will begin to reflect more of what they are learning.

MC Gathering Review —

What went well? What would you do differently next time?
What are you learning about leading a MC?

_____

_____

_____

_____

_____

_____

_____

_____

_____

_____

_____

_____

_____

_____

_____

_____

MC Gathering Review —

What went well? What would you do differently next time?
What are you learning about leading a MC?

_____

_____

_____

_____

_____

_____

_____

_____

_____

_____

_____

_____

_____

_____

_____

Week 2 Summary

☑ UP/IN Gathering
☑ Small Groups — Understanding Dad

MC Schedule

■ Eat (30 minutes)

_____

_____

_____

_____

_____

■ Thanksgiving (15 minutes)

_____

_____

_____

_____

_____

■ Singing/Worship (15 minutes)

_____

_____

_____

_____

_____

■ Small Groups (20 minutes)

—Small Group (20 min) _____

_____

_____

_____

_____

■ Prayer (10 minutes)

—Prayer (10 min) _____

_____

_____

_____

_____

Leader Tips

■ Small Groups — Understanding Dad
- God is both our Dad and the King of the universe. That's amazing! He wants to hang with us at the dinner table, and he also invites us to join him in ruling the earth (Genesis 1:26-28[20]). He loves us and cares for us, but he also has a day job.
- We all have developed different views of God and how we're supposed to talk with him. These have been shaped by our church experiences, what we learned from other family and friends, and especially by our own relationship (or lack of relationship) with our fathers. Some of us engage God as Father, but find it difficult to see him as King. We love his provision for us, but not his

---

[20] Read Covenant & Kingdom for a greater explanation, Breen

lordship. Others see God only as King and Lord and have a deep respect for him, but do not experience the gentle ways of God as Father.

- Which aspect of God do we lean toward? How is this a reflection of what we have experienced and learned in the past? Are we open to growing in how we engage God as both Dad and King?
- (20 minutes) Send the MC into small groups to share and pray for each other.

■ Debrief
- Gather everyone back together and invite people to share where they have grown. Take time to affirm people, and also don't be afraid to point out where you as the leaders have seen different people grow.

MC Gathering Review –

What went well? What would you do differently next time?
What are you learning about leading a MC?

_____

_____

_____

_____

_____

_____

_____

_____

_____

_____

_____

_____

_____

_____

Week 3 Summary

☑ UP/IN Gathering
☑ Small Groups — SG Questions or Other

MC Schedule

◼ Eat (30 minutes)

_____
_____
_____
_____
_____

◼ Thanksgiving (15 minutes)

_____
_____
_____
_____

◼ Singing/Worship (15 minutes)

_____
_____
_____
_____
_____

■ Small Groups (20 minutes)

Small Group (20 min)

_____

_____

_____

_____

_____

■ Prayer (10 minutes)

Prayer (10 min)

_____

_____

_____

_____

_____

Leader Tips

■ Small Groups
  - Use the Small Group Questions in the appendix. Make enough copies to share one sheet with each SG, and pass the sheets out as they go into SGs.
  - We instruct members of our MC to get into groups of 3-4 and go through as many of the questions as they have time for.
  - If you have a core team you are discipling and enough to divide the group, then have them raise their hands and let 2-3 others gather with them. They can be your SG leaders. You can encourage these leaders be consistent each time or allow people to gather spontaneously with a different group each time, depending on which seems to work better for your group.

■ Debrief
  ▪ Leave 10 minutes at the end of your time together to regroup and share anything from SG that the rest of the family needs to know about. Maybe someone is celebrating a new job or has just found out they have a physical illness or are in need of a new job.
  ▪ We strongly encourage that people share for themselves and not for others. If they say they have permission to share for someone else, I always verify with that person on the spot first.
  ▪ We often take time to quickly pray for some of the things shared in this setting.

MC Gathering Review –

What went well? What would you do differently next time?

_____

_____

_____

_____

_____

_____

_____

_____

_____

_____

_____

_____

_____

_____

_____

_____

Week 4 Summary

☑ IN/OUT Gathering
☑ OUT Adventure/Mission Vision

MC Schedule

■ You may choose to engage your OUT activity during the usual
time of your UP/IN gath-erings, or it may make more sense to do it
on a different day of the week. During one season our MC met on
Wednesday evenings, and our OUT activities were better en-gaged
on the weekends, so that's what we did. On our IN/OUT weeks we
have often moved our gathering time to the day/time that was most
conducive to our OUT activity.

■ Of course, an OUT gathering your schedule will look different than
your UP/IN gather-ings. We recommend you gather together first to
give clear instruction for the activity and also provide a few minutes
on the back end to debrief your experience.
- Gather for instruction.
- Engage your Mission Vision (we discuss this fully in Part 1 under
  IN/OUT Rhythms).
- Take a few minutes after the activity or at your next MC gathering
  to debrief the OUT experience with your MC.

Leader Tips

- We offer lots of ideas in the Appendix that you can try and experiment with. You'll also want to make sure you are throwing a party at least once a month as well. This gives you a minimum of two OUT activities per month. You may do more, but two is a good starting point, especially for those for whom the OUT dimension is more challenging. Remember, predictable patterns like this will create a new culture in your heart and your MC.

- Make sure to clearly communicate to your MC ahead of time what activity you will be engaging. Does the activity require special accessories like:
  - Walking shoes for a prayer walk
  - Paint brushes, rollers, etc for painting
  - Clean or dirty clothes
  - Games for a party

- Be appreciative and empathetic with those who are uncomfortable about the OUT activity. Gently encourage them join you, even if they only watch or take a more passive or quiet role. You're helping everyone grow in the OUT dimension, but we have to begin where people are, not where we wish they were.

- Be sensitive to the physical limitations for different OUT activities and consider whether you will be excluding members of your MC in an activity. Perhaps they can provide prayer support onsite or just a friendly smile to those you are serving.

  Kids: Be sensitive to the ages of your MC's kids and how they can engage with your OUT activity.

MC Gathering Review —

What went well? What would you do differently next time?

_____

_____

_____

_____

_____

_____

_____

_____

_____

_____

_____

_____

_____

_____

Week 1 Summary

☑ UP/IN Gathering
☑ Family Devotion — What is God Saying and Doing?
— PART 1

MC Schedule

◼ Eat (30 minutes)

_____
_____
_____
_____
_____

◼ Thanksgiving (15 minutes)

_____
_____
_____
_____
_____

◼ Singing/Worship (15 minutes)

_____
_____
_____
_____
_____

■ Family Devotion (20 minutes)

Small Group (20 min)

_____

_____

_____

_____

_____

■ Prayer (10 minutes)

Prayer (10 min)

_____

_____

_____

_____

_____

Leader Tips

■ Family Devotion — What is God Saying and Doing? — PART 1

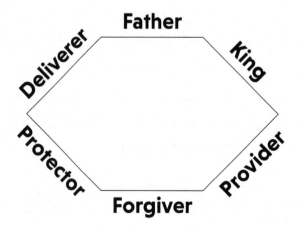

- (5 minutes) — Remind your MC of the Hexagon as a tool that helps us remember who God is as we draw near to him in prayer.

Jesus taught his disciples, "This is how you should pray." Even more, this is how Jesus trained his disciples to engage the Father for EVERYTHING in their lives.

- (15 minutes) Give the MC a moment to think of something that is on each person's heart for prayer. Take time individually and silently to filter this prayer need through each of the six phrases of the Lord's prayer, listening to what God may be saying or showing you. For example, if your prayer need is a new job, then begin by reflecting on who God is as Father and what your Father might be saying and doing in relation to your need for a new job. Do the same for each of the other five phrases.
- Feel free to encourage people to spread out and find somewhere more comfortable to do this.
- (10 minutes) Gather the group again and invite people to share anything they heard God saying or doing. Remind them that this is just practice, and that MC needs to be a safe place for everyone to grow and learn together.
- You will want to be very invitational and celebrate what is shared, as this may be a vulnerable experience for some in the group. Be careful not to lift up certain things shared because they sound better or more spiritual.

- You can illustrate the Lord's prayer like a funnel that we are filtering our prayer needs through. Explain to the group that what comes out will be different than what goes in, since it has been filtered by who God is. I may pour in anxiety, but come out with peace. I may pour in ambiguity about a decision, and come out with clarity or a way forward.

MC Gathering Review –

What went well? What would you do differently next time?
What are you learning about leading a MC?

_____

_____

_____

_____

_____

_____

_____

_____

_____

_____

_____

_____

_____

_____

_____

Interval 11 — Engaging God

Week 2 Summary

☑ UP/IN Gathering
☑ Small Groups — Prayer Filtering

MC Schedule

■ Eat (30 minutes)

Eat (30 min)

_____
_____
_____
_____
_____

■ Thanksgiving (15 minutes)

Thanksgiving (15 min)

_____
_____
_____
_____
_____

■ Singing/Worship (15 minutes)

Worship (15 min)

_____
_____
_____
_____
_____

■ Small Groups (20 minutes)

■ **Small Group** (20 min) _____

_____

_____

_____

■ Prayer (10 minutes)

■ **Prayer** (10 min) _____

_____

_____

_____

Leader Tips

■ Small Groups — Prayer Filtering
  ▪ (20 minutes) Send the MC into small groups to practice the same **prayer filtering** exercise you did together during your last gathering. This time people are going to learn how to filter someone else's prayer need. Instructions:.
    ▪ Pick one person who will share a prayer need.
    ▪ Take five minutes for everyone to quietly filter that person's prayer need through the Lord's prayer.
    ▪ Take 3-5 minutes for everyone to share with that person what you hear the Lord saying and doing. Remind them that we're practicing, so some things will stick and be helpful while others may not—and that's OK!
    ▪ Give the person an opportunity to share what they connect with.

- Finish by praying a blessing over that person.

- Debrief
  - Gather everyone back and invite them to share their experiences in their small groups. What most grabbed their attention?

MC Gathering Review –

What went well? What would you do differently next time?
What are you learning about leading a MC?

_____

_____

_____

_____

_____

_____

_____

_____

_____

_____

_____

_____

_____

_____

_____

_____

Week 3 Summary

- ☑ UP/IN Gathering
- ☑ Small Groups — SG Questions or Other

MC Schedule

■ Eat (30 minutes)

_____

_____

_____

_____

_____

■ Thanksgiving (15 minutes)

_____

_____

_____

_____

_____

■ Singing/Worship (15 minutes)

_____

_____

_____

_____

_____

■ Small Groups (20 minutes)

Small Group (20 min) _____
_____

_____

_____

_____

■ Prayer (10 minutes)

Prayer (10 min) _____
_____

_____

_____

_____

Leader Tips

■ Small Groups
  - Use the Small Group Questions in the appendix. Make enough copies to share one sheet with each SG, and pass the sheets out as they go into SGs.
  - We instruct members of our MC to get into groups of 3-4 and go through as many of the questions as they have time for.
  - If you have a core team you are discipling and enough to divide the group, then have them raise their hands and let 2-3 others gather with them. They can be your SG leaders. You can encourage these leaders be consistent each time or allow people to gather spontaneously with a different group each time, depending on which seems to work better for your group

- Debrief
  - Leave 10 minutes at the end of your time together to regroup and share anything from SG that the rest of the family needs to know about. Maybe someone is celebrating a new job or has just found out they have a physical illness or are in need of a new job.
  - We strongly encourage that people share for themselves and not for others. If they say they have permission to share for someone else, I always verify with that person on the spot first.
  - We often take time to quickly pray for some of the things shared in this setting.

MC Gathering Review —

What went well? What would you do differently next time?

_____

_____

_____

_____

_____

_____

_____

_____

_____

_____

_____

_____

_____

Week 4 Summary

- ☑ IN/OUT Gathering
- ☑ OUT Adventure/Mission Vision

MC Schedule

- ■ You may choose to engage your OUT activity during the usual time of your UP/IN gatherings, or it may make more sense to do it on a different day of the week. During one season our MC met on Wednesday evenings, and our OUT activities were better engaged on the weekends, so that's what we did. On our IN/OUT weeks we have often moved our gathering time to the day/time that was most conducive to our OUT activity.

- ■ Of course, an OUT gathering your schedule will look different than your UP/IN gatherings. We recommend you gather together first to give clear instruction for the activity and also provide a few minutes on the back end to debrief your experience.
  - ▪ Gather for instruction.
  - ▪ Engage your Mission Vision (we discuss this fully in Part 1 under IN/OUT Rhythms).
  - ▪ Take a few minutes after the activity or at your next MC gathering to debrief the OUT experience with your MC.

Leader Tips

■ We offer lots of ideas in the Appendix that you can try and experiment with. You'll also want to make sure you are throwing a party at least once a month as well. This gives you a minimum of two OUT activities per month. You may do more, but two is a good starting point, especially for those for whom the OUT dimension is more challenging. Remember, predictable patterns like this will create a new culture in your heart and your MC.

■ Make sure to clearly communicate to your MC ahead of time what activity you will be engaging. Does the activity require special accessories like:
  - Walking shoes for a prayer walk
  - Paint brushes, rollers, etc for painting
  - Clean or dirty clothes
  - Games for a party

■ Be appreciative and empathetic with those who are uncomfortable about the OUT activity. Gently encourage them join you, even if they only watch or take a more passive or quiet role. You're helping everyone grow in the OUT dimension, but we have to begin where people are, not where we wish they were.

■ Be sensitive to the physical limitations for different OUT activities and consider whether you will be excluding members of your MC in an activity. Perhaps they can provide prayer support onsite or just a friendly smile to those you are serving.

Kids: Be sensitive to the ages of your MC's kids and how they can engage with your OUT activity.

MC Gathering Review —

What went well? What would you do differently next time?

_____

_____

_____

_____

_____

_____

_____

_____

_____

_____

_____

_____

_____

_____

_____

_____

_____

Interval 12 — Engaging God

Week 1 Summary

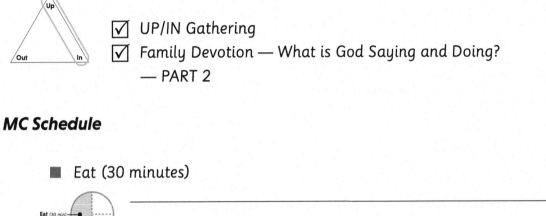

☑ UP/IN Gathering
☑ Family Devotion — What is God Saying and Doing?
   — PART 2

MC Schedule

■ Eat (30 minutes)

_____
_____
_____
_____

■ Thanksgiving (15 minutes)

_____
_____
_____
_____

■ Singing/Worship (15 minutes)

_____
_____
_____
_____

- ■ Family Devotion (20 minutes)

    ◖ ●—**Small Group** (20 min) _____

    _____

    _____

    _____

    _____

- ■ Prayer (10 minutes)

    ◖ ●—**Prayer** (10 min) _____

    _____

    _____

    _____

    _____

Leader Tips

- ■ Family Devotion — What is God Saying and Doing? — Part 2
    - ■ Most of us have learned to ask God for what we want or need. But we also need to remember that God has a lot on his heart to share with us. The many pages of scripture and the way Jesus invested in his disciples reveal to us that God loves to share his heart and mind with us. We need to take time to listen.
    - ■ (20 minutes total) Remind your MC of the Hexagon and let them know you will be engaging in a new exercise utilizing this helpful visual tool. This exercise is called **listening prayer**. Instead of filtering a specific prayer need through the Lord's Prayer, we're going to take a couple minutes to simply reflect on each of the six phrases of the Lord's Prayer, listening for anything the Lord may want to speak to us. Let them know that they may hear more in one of the phrases than the others, and that's OK. This exercise is

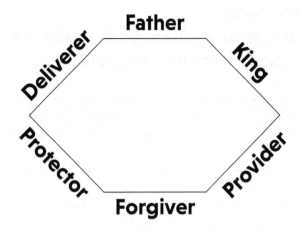

a simple, repeatable way of making room for what God is trying to say to us at any given moment.

- (5 minutes) Introduce the listening prayer exercise.
- (12 minutes) Give the group two minutes to listen through each phrase.
- (3 minutes) Gather everyone back together and give them a chance to share what they are hearing.

MC Gathering Review —

What went well? What would you do differently next time?
What are you learning about leading a MC?

_____

_____

_____

_____

_____

_____

_____

_____

_____

_____

_____

_____

_____

_____

Week 2 Summary

☑ UP/IN Gathering
☑ Small Groups — Listening Prayer for Each Other

MC Schedule

■ Eat (30 minutes)

_____
_____
_____
_____

■ Thanksgiving (15 minutes)

_____
_____
_____
_____
_____

■ Singing/Worship (15 minutes)

_____
_____
_____
_____
_____

■ Small Groups (20 minutes)

- Small Group (20 min) _____

_____

_____

_____

_____

■ Prayer (10 minutes)

- Prayer (10 min) _____

_____

_____

_____

_____

Leader Tips

■ Small Groups — Listening Prayer for Each Other
  - (20 minutes) Send people into SGs with the following instructions:
    - Choose one person in your SG to pray for. Take 3-5 few minutes to listen to God for that person using the Lord's Prayer. As we talked about last week, this is called Listening Prayer.
    - After a few minutes, share with that person what you heard from the Lord. Remind everyone that we never hear perfectly from the Lord so we have to weigh what is shared by allowing God to confirm what has been shared.
    - Ask the person whether they connect with anything being shared, and if so, why.
    - Gather everyone back together to debrief.

■ Debrief

  ▪ Gather everyone back and invite them to share their experiences in their small groups. What most grabbed their attention?

MC Gathering Review –

What went well? What would you do differently next time?
What are you learning about leading a MC?

_____

_____

_____

_____

_____

_____

_____

_____

_____

_____

_____

_____

_____

_____

_____

_____

Week 3 Summary

☑ UP/IN Gathering
☑ Small Groups — SG Questions or Other

MC Schedule

◼ Eat (30 minutes)

Eat (30 min)

_____

_____

_____

_____

◼ Thanksgiving (15 minutes)

Thanksgiving (15 min)

_____

_____

_____

_____

◼ Singing/Worship (15 minutes)

Worship (15 min)

_____

_____

_____

_____

■ Small Groups (20 minutes)

Small Group (20 min) _____

_____

_____

_____

■ Prayer (10 minutes)

Prayer (10 min) _____

_____

_____

_____

Leader Tips

■ Small Groups
  - Use the Small Group Questions in the appendix. Make enough copies to share one sheet with each SG, and pass the sheets out as they go into SGs.
  - We instruct members of our MC to get into groups of 3-4 and go through as many of the questions as they have time for.
  - If you have a core team you are discipling and enough to divide the group, then have them raise their hands and let 2-3 others gather with them. They can be your SG leaders. You can encourage these leaders be consistent each time or allow people to gather spontaneously with a different group each time, depending on which seems to work better for your group.

■ Debrief
  ▪ Leave 10 minutes at the end of your time together to regroup and share anything from SG that the rest of the family needs to know about. Maybe someone is celebrating a new job or has just found out they have a physical illness or are in need of a new job.
  ▪ We strongly encourage that people share for themselves and not for others. If they say they have permission to share for someone else, I always verify with that person on the spot first.
  ▪ We often take time to quickly pray for some of the things shared in this setting.

MC Gathering Review –

What went well? What would you do differently next time?

_____

_____

_____

_____

_____

_____

_____

_____

_____

_____

_____

_____

_____

_____

_____

Week 4 Summary

☑ IN/OUT Gathering
☑ OUT Adventure/Mission Vision

MC Schedule

■ You may choose to engage your OUT activity during the usual time of your UP/IN gatherings, or it may make more sense to do it on a different day of the week. During one season our MC met on Wednesday evenings, and our OUT activities were better engaged on the weekends, so that's what we did. On our IN/OUT weeks we have often moved our gathering time to the day/time that was most conducive to our OUT activity.

■ Of course, an OUT gathering your schedule will look different than your UP/IN gatherings. We recommend you gather together first to give clear instruction for the activity and also provide a few minutes on the back end to debrief your experience.
  - Gather for instruction.
  - Engage your Mission Vision (we discuss this fully in Part 1 under IN/OUT Rhythms).
  - Take a few minutes after the activity or at your next MC gathering to debrief the OUT experience with your MC.

Leader Tips

■ We offer lots of ideas in the Appendix that you can try and experiment with. You'll also want to make sure you are throwing a party at least once a month as well. This gives you a minimum of two OUT activities per month. You may do more, but two is a good starting point, especially for those for whom the OUT dimension is more challenging. Remember, predictable patterns like this will create a new culture in your heart and your MC.

■ Make sure to clearly communicate to your MC ahead of time what activity you will be engaging. Does the activity require special accessories like:
  - Walking shoes for a prayer walk
  - Paint brushes, rollers, etc for painting
  - Clean or dirty clothes
  - Games for a party

■ Be appreciative and empathetic with those who are uncomfortable about the OUT activity. Gently encourage them join you, even if they only watch or take a more passive or quiet role. You're helping everyone grow in the OUT dimension, but we have to begin where people are, not where we wish they were.

■ Be sensitive to the physical limitations for different OUT activities and consider whether you will be excluding members of your MC in an activity. Perhaps they can provide prayer support onsite or just a friendly smile to those you are serving.

  Kids: Be sensitive to the ages of your MC's kids and how they can engage with your OUT activity.

MC Gathering Review —

What went well? What would you do differently next time?

_____

_____

_____

_____

_____

_____

_____

_____

_____

_____

_____

_____

_____

_____

_____

_____

_____

MC ASSESSMENT EXERCISE UP, IN, OUT Triangle Assessment

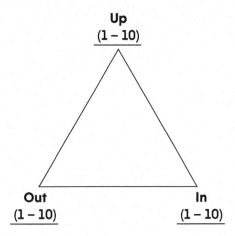

(1) Have each member of your team score your MC 1-10 for each of the 3 dimensions.

(2) Have each member share and explain their results. Then process as a team what there is to learn from what is being shared.

(3) Here are some helpful questions to reflect on after you have processed everyone's scores:

- ■ Maintain — What do we need to keep doing that is going well?
- ■ Margin — Where do we need to create space in our MC for new things?
- ■ Maximize — What are we already doing that needs greater intentionality?
- ■ Move into — What do we need to start doing?

Remember, this is a framework in which there is freedom to experiment with and integrate into your MC new activities that may be irregular or regular. Feel free to draw on ideas from the Appendix or others that you have learned. The journey of learning the MC lifestyle is not one of success and failure, but rather of process and learning.

APPENDIX

Small Group Activities for UP/IN Gatherings

Small Group Questions for MC.

■ We recommend you print these questions for your group and use them during the fourth week of the MC Framework each month. Remember, get through as many as you have time for. There's no need to hurry.

- What are you thankful for (People share)
- Is anyone sick? (Discuss. Pray for them.)
- Is anyone anxious or worried? (Discuss. Pray for them.)
- Are there any Persons of Peace on our hearts? (Discuss. Pray for them.)
- What does our community need? (Discuss. Pray for it.)

More ideas for SGs

■ Rate yourself 1-10 for each dimension of the UP, IN, OUT Triangle. Celebrate your high score and pray for your low score.

■ Share one area where you're finding it difficult to have a good attitude. (Discuss. Pray for them.)

■ Share one person you are praying becomes a Christian. (Discuss. Pray for them.)

■ Who is one neighbor you are going to commit to praying for? (Discuss. Pray for them.)

TEMPLATE MC OUTLINES

Week 1

☑ UP/IN Gathering
☑ Family Devotional

MC Schedule

■ Eat (30 minutes)

Eat (30 min)

_____
_____
_____
_____
_____

■ Thanksgiving (15 minutes)

Thanksgiving (15 min)

_____
_____
_____
_____
_____

■ Singing/Worship (15 minutes)

Worship (15 min)

_____
_____
_____
_____
_____

■ Family Devotion (20 minutes)

Small Group (20 min)
_____
_____
_____
_____
_____

■ Prayer (10 minutes)

Prayer (10 min)
_____
_____
_____
_____
_____

Leader Tips

■ Family Devotion
- What do you think you need to invest into your MC in this season? Remember, it's not about being an amazing teacher, but about helping your MC operate more and more like a Family on Mission.
- You can invite others in your MC to share what they are learning from God. We have often taken the 20 minutes and opened the floor to anyone who wanted to share in 2-3 minutes what they have been learning from God.
- This is a great time to show short videos that may be helpful for your MC.
- It's a good idea to always leave a few minutes at the end of your Family Devotional for some Discussion and Q&A.

MC Gathering Review –

What went well? What would you do differently next time?
What are you learning about leading a MC?

_____

_____

_____

_____

_____

_____

_____

_____

_____

_____

_____

_____

_____

_____

_____

_____

_____

_____

_____

Week 2

- ☑ UP/IN Gathering
- ☑ Small Groups

MC Schedule

▪ Eat (30 minutes)

Eat (30 min)

_____

_____

_____

_____

_____

▪ Thanksgiving (15 minutes)

Thanksgiving (15 min)

_____

_____

_____

_____

_____

▪ Singing/Worship (15 minutes)

Worship (15 min)

_____

_____

_____

_____

_____

■ **Small Groups (20 minutes)**

○—Small Group (20 min) _____

_____

_____

_____

_____

■ **Prayer (10 minutes)**

○—Prayer (10 min) _____

_____

_____

_____

_____

Leader Tips

■ Small Groups
  - We have found it very helpful to follow up a week of Family Devotion with a Small Group time that helps your MC process and pray about what you have shared with them. An easy way to do this is to simply remind them of what was shared the week prior and to share in small group what most grabbed their attention.
  - Otherwise, you can utilize any of the small group activities in the Appendix.

■ Debrief
  - Don't forget to gather everyone back and invite them to share their experiences in their small groups. What most grabbed their attention? This gives you an opportunity to speak into the different questions and reflections that come up.

MC Gathering Review –

What went well? What would you do differently next time?
What are you learning about leading a MC?

_____

_____

_____

_____

_____

_____

_____

_____

_____

_____

_____

_____

_____

_____

_____

Week 3

☑ UP/IN Gathering
☑ Small Groups — SG Questions or Other

MC Schedule

■ Eat (30 minutes)

Eat (30 min)

_____

_____

_____

_____

_____

■ Thanksgiving (15 minutes)

Thanksgiving (15 min)

_____

_____

_____

_____

■ Singing/Worship (15 minutes)

Worship (15 min)

_____

_____

_____

_____

_____

■ Small Groups (20 minutes)

    Small Group (20 min)

    _____

    _____

_____

_____

_____

■ Prayer (10 minutes)

    Prayer (10 min)

    _____

    _____

_____

_____

_____

Leader Tips

■ Small Groups
- You can use the Small Group Questions in the appendix or experiment with other activities from the Appendix on Small Group Activities.
- Instruct your MC to get into groups of 3-4 and offer them clear instruction on what they are doing.

■ Debrief
- Leave 10 minutes at the end of your time to gather everyone and hear anything from small groups that the rest of the family needs to hear about or be aware of.

MC Gathering Review —

What went well? What would you do differently next time?
What are you learning about leading a MC?

_____

_____

_____

_____

_____

_____

_____

_____

_____

_____

_____

_____

_____

_____

_____

_____

Week 4

 ☑ IN/OUT Gathering

MC Schedule

■ You may choose to engage your OUT activity during the usual time of your UP/IN gatherings, or it may make more sense to do it on a different day of the week. During one season our MC met on Wednesday evenings, and our OUT activities were better engaged on the weekends, so that's what we did. On our IN/OUT weeks we have often moved our gathering time to the day/time that was most conducive to our OUT activity.

■ Of course, an OUT gathering your schedule will look different than your UP/IN gatherings. We recommend you gather together first to give clear instruction for the activity and also provide a few minutes on the back end to debrief your experience.
  - Gather for instruction.
  - Engage your Mission Vision (we discuss this fully in Part 1 under IN/OUT Rhythms).
  - Take a few minutes after the activity or at your next MC gathering to debrief the OUT experience with your MC.

Leader Tips

■ We offer lots of ideas in the Appendix that you can try and experiment with. You'll also want to make sure you are throwing a party at least once a month as well. This gives you a minimum of two OUT activities per month. You may do more, but two is a good starting point, especially for those for whom the OUT dimension is more challenging. Remember, predictable patterns like this will create a new culture in your heart and your MC.

■ Make sure to clearly communicate to your MC ahead of time what activity you will be engaging. Does the activity require special accessories like:
  - Walking shoes for a prayer walk
  - Paint brushes, rollers, etc for painting
  - Clean or dirty clothes
  - Games for a party

■ Be appreciative and empathetic with those who are uncomfortable about the OUT activity. Gently encourage them join you, even if they only watch or take a more passive or quiet role. You're helping everyone grow in the OUT dimension, but we have to begin where people are, not where we wish they were.

■ Be sensitive to the physical limitations for different OUT activities and consider whether you will be excluding members of your MC in an activity. Perhaps they can provide prayer support onsite or just a friendly smile to those you are serving.

Kids: Be sensitive to the ages of your MC's kids and how they can engage with your OUT activity.

MC Gathering Review –

What went well? What would you do differently next time?

_____

_____

_____

_____

_____

_____

_____

_____

_____

_____

_____

_____

_____

_____

_____

_____

_____

Growing Your UP, IN, OUT

Growing your UP:

- Commit to a common Bible reading plan. We utilize the Moravian Texts: http://www.moravian.org/faith-a-congregations/an-introduction-to-the-daily-texts-2/

- Commit to a common prayer tactic.
    - You can post the prayer needs of the community or of your POPs to a private Facebook page.
    - You can also commit to praying the Psalms together on a daily basis.

- Some of the activities suggested for Growing your In would apply here also
    - Host a night of worship and prayer with the focus being caring for one another
    - Start a prayer board for your MC — Pin specific prayers to the board and commit to praying for them until the prayers are answered. Replace answered prayers with new ones. You can even post these prayers on a private Facebook page.

- Watch a video sermon together and discuss afterwards.

- Attend a conference or seminar together that addresses your relationship with God.

■ Identify three things in your community that seem impossible to change for better, and commit as a MC to praying for them until something begins to move.

■ Invite everyone to read a book on prayer, engaging the Holy Spirit, or another topic in our spare time. Host a gathering to discuss what you're learning.

■ Keep a MC testimony journal. Encourage your MC participants to write their testimonies in a journal that you read back to them from time to time.

Growing your IN:

■ Host a night of worship and prayer with the focus being caring for one another

■ Start a prayer board for your MC — Pin specific prayers to the board and commit to praying for them until the prayers are answered. Replace answered prayers with new ones. You can even post these prayers on a private Facebook page.

■ Take up offerings for those who have financial needs.

■ Date night/Adult night out — Have a date night where the teenagers or single adults watch the kids while the couples go out for dinner and a movie together. You can also pitch in for babysitting and have all the adults go out together.

■ Take a camping trip together.

■ Find out the different hobbies represented in your MC and create opportunities for people to try a new hobby with members of your MC.

■ Go to a family movie with all the kids!

■ Go on a spiritual retreat for a day or two. You can either host your own or research an organization that specializes in this.

■ Find a way for your MC to serve another MC or a particular need discovered within your church community.

■ Send the ladies for a manicure/pedicure/spa treatment.

■ Send the gentlemen for a day of fishing or the like.

Growing your OUT:

■ Prayer Walking
  ■ Prayer walks are great ways to include kids, as long as you have considered the safety of the area, streets, sidewalks, etc.
  ■ Places to prayer walk:
    ■ Your neighborhood
    ■ Neighborhood, street, area you feel called to
    ■ Mall, business complex
    ■ Strip mall, etc.

■ Places of Recreation
  ■ Consider where you live and think of places people like to gather for recreation and decide on somewhere you're going to begin gathering there when possible as a MC. You can host BBQs,

picnics, outdoor games, etc. These places may include:

- Parks
- Beaches
- Trail hikes
- Lakes, etc.

- Hobbies
  - Reach out to those who share a common hobby. There are as many different hobbies as there are people it seems. Some of these may include:
    - Golf communities
    - Adult and youth sports leagues
    - Families involved in youth sports
    - Dart-throwing clubs
    - Crossfit gyms
    - Remote Control cars, boats, planes. etc.
    - Community garden

- Host an Alpha Course[21]
  - We have experienced great success when MCs have hosted the Alpha Course, because the MC becomes the natural community participants will continue with.
  - We have seen MCs grow and multiply while hosting Alpha Courses.

- Invite friends to join you for a journey through the Story of God[22]
  - The Story of God is a great way for both your MC and guests

---

[21] AlphaUSA.org

[22] Story of God, Caesar Kalinowski

---

to engage the story of the Bible in a way that puts everyone on equal footing. You simply read a story representing a portion of the scripture and then ask the facilitator questions. Everyone gets to play!

- Throw Parties for any reason:
  - Super Bowl or other sporting events that people gather around
  - Community Easter Egg hunt
  - Christmas Party
  - Halloween Party
  - Etc

- Host a Movie night — You'll have to be careful about what movie you show based on who is planning on attending, but these can be lots of fun. You can even provide popcorn and drinks.

- Participate in local city activities
  - You may have to dig around a bit, but you can find opportunities online with a bit of research.
  - Most local coffee houses have bulletin boards with local activities.
  - Engage in local parades, festivals, celebrations, etc. Join the party where it's al-ready happening!
  - Many schools have after-school programs and need lots of help.

Missional Purpose Activity Sheets

....

....

....

....

Passions

Problems   Possessions

....

....

....

....

Missional Purpose Activity Sheets

....

....

....

....

Passions

Problems   Possessions

....

....

....

....

Missional Purpose Activity Sheets

....
....
....
....

Passions

Problems   Possessions

....
....
....
....

Missional Purpose Activity Sheets

....

....

....

....

Passions

Problems   Possessions

....

....

....

....

Missional Purpose Activity Sheets

....
....
....
....

Passions

Problems   Possessions

....
....
....
....

Missional Purpose Activity Sheets

....

....

....

....

Passions

```
        /\
       /  \
      /    \
     /      \
    /        \
   /          \
  /            \
 /_____\
```

Problems   Possessions

....

....

....

....

MC ASSESSMENT EXERCISE UP, IN, OUT Triangle Assessment

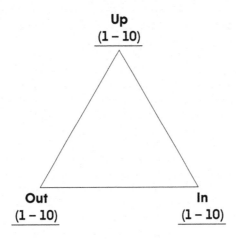

(1) Have each member of your team score your MC 1-10 for each of the 3 dimensions.

(2) Have each member share and explain their results. Then process as a team what there is to learn from what is being shared.

(3) Here are some helpful questions to reflect on after you have processed everyone's scores:

- Maintain — What do we need to keep doing that is going well?
- Margin — Where do we need to create space in our MC for new things?
- Maximize — What are we already doing that needs greater intentionality?
- Move into — What do we need to start doing?

Remember, this is a framework in which there is freedom to experiment with and integrate into your MC new activities that may be irregular or regular. Feel free to draw on ideas from the Appendix or others that you have learned. The journey of learning the MC lifestyle is not one of success and failure, but rather of process and learning.

CPSIA information can be obtained
at www.ICGtesting.com
Printed in the USA
LVOW04s1230140817
544948LV00015B/738/P

9 780996 530095